LIFE, SCIENCE, AND ART

Being LEAVES FROM ERNEST HELLO.

Translated from the French by E. M. WALKER.

Introduction with notes by Gary Furnell

Connor Court Publishing

Copyright © Introduction, Notes, Gary Furnell, 2025.

First published by R. & T. Washborne, Paternoster Row, London, 1912.

All rights reserved. No part of this book may be reproduced or transmitted in any form or by any means, electronic or mechanical, including photo copying, recording or by any information storage and retrieval system, without prior permission in writing from the publisher.

Connor Court Publishing Pty Ltd
PO Box 7257
Redland Bay QLD 4165
sales@connorcourt.com
www.connorcourt.com
Phone 0497-900-685

Printed and bound in Australia.

ISBN: 9781923224643

Cover design: Tim Jones.
Cover images: 'Angelus' by J.F. Millet; a19th Century microscope; a potrait of Ernest Hello: digitally enhanced.

The Philosophical Notes
No. 4

PREVIOUS VOLUMES

No.1
The Evolution of Evolution by St. George Jackson Mivart
Introduced and edited by Gary Furnell

No.2
That Which is Seen and That Which is Not Seen together with What is Government? and Petition of the Candlemakers by Frédéric Bastiat
Introduced and edited by Gary Furnell
Foreword by Peter Fenwick

No. 3
Instructions for Politicians: The Best of Edmund Burke
Introduced and edited by Gary Furnell
Foreword by Hon. Kevin Andrews

I have tried to show how Life, Science, and Art are three mirrors, each of which reflects the same face.

ERNEST HELLO

CONTENTS

INTRODUCTION TO THE PHILOSOPHICAL NOTES EDITION		9
TRANSLATOR'S NOTE TO THE ORIGINAL EDITION		13
I.	The One Thing Necessary	21
II.	The Sphinx	25
III.	Intellectual Charity	28
IV.	Some Considerations on Charity	33
V.	Great Men	35
VI.	No Time!	39
VII.	Isolation and Solitude	41
VIII.	Hope	43
IX.	Unity	47
X.	The Spirit of Contradiction	50
XI.	Appearance and Reality	54
XII.	Indifference	58
XIII.	Light and the People	61
XIV.	The Age and the Ages	64
XV.	Contemplatives and Lunatics	68
XVI.	The World	71
XVII.	The Mediocre Man	74
XVIII.	Envy	76
XIX.	On the False Association of Ideas	79
XX.	Art	81
XXI.	Contempt for Art	83
XXII.	The Ridiculous	85
XXIII.	The Press	87
XXIV.	History	93
XXV.	Science	97
XXVI.	The Holy Scriptures	99
XXVII.	The Holy Angels	102
XXVIII.	Alone and Poor	106
XXIX.	The Friends of Job	107
XXX.	"Credo, Domine, Adjuva Incredulitatem meam"	108
XXXI.	Work and Rest	112

Introduction

In the third essay, *Intellectual Charity*, of this collection we read:

> Now, written speech may be a great charity, and its diffusion, whenever it is true and beautiful, is one of the acts of charity most suited to our time. In many souls, a hunger and thirst exists which can only be satisfied by printed words. Between these eager readers and the writer (who should also be eager) a current of sublime charity may be established, since all give and all receive.

The reason for this reprint is to satisfy, in some small measure, that intellectual hunger and thirst with the beauty of revealed and natural truth in printed form. The need for this type of life-enriching charity is as desperate today as it was 150 years ago when Hello wrote those words.

Ernest Hello (1828-1885) was a French journalist. Along with his journalism, he published several books of criticism and philosophy. *Life, Science and Art* forms a valuable introduction to his writing and thought. This work has not been published in English, in a new edition, for over one hundred years.

Hello understood that an accessible, engaging style attracted readers. He was sensitive to literature and art, and he wrote in a manner that embedded timeless aphorisms in articles that have been overlooked. He was not long-winded. Perhaps his journalistic training alerted him to the merit of brevity. Certainly, the pieces collected here have focused brevity—large ideas are encapsulated in, at most, five or six pages.

Ernest Hello's near-contemporary, philosopher Soren Kierkegaard, complained that journalists emphasised temporal matters to the exclusion of eternal, spiritual concerns. There are, fortunately, exceptions to this rule and Ernest Hello is exceptional. A devout Catholic, he critiqued his age—a time of accelerating modernity, politely dismissive of Judeo-Christian values—and warned that it would become confused, irrational, unhappy and fastidious about faddish values.

He saw long-standing, functional religious customs, values and ideas dismantled to allow, supposedly, human flourishing under the aegis of triumphant science and liberal politics. He disliked this aspect of his era and argued against the delusion of assuming that temporal imperatives were more important than divine imperatives.

Hello's Catholic perspective gives *Life, Science and Art* a prophetic quality. Not in the sense of foretelling, but through forthright truth-telling.

Words and ideas—the thoughtful journalist's tools of trade—were important to Hello. He highlighted the importance of truthful, well-chosen words in the chapters *The Spirit of Contradiction, Some Considerations on Charity*, and *The Press*.

He wanted ideas articulated and examined and then adopted if logical and worthy, or discarded if illogical and worthless. He emphasised thinking about ideas in the chapters *Light and the People, The Age and the Ages*, and *Contemplatives and Lunatics*.

Hello insisted that God and Truth were a unity and therefore any attempt to separate the divine from the temporal was bound to fail. The firmer the separation, the greater the disaster. He explored this separation in the chapters *The One Thing Necessary, Appearance and Reality, Science* and *The World*. After two world wars, a multitude of murderous totalitarian states and now an alarming rise in family breakdown together with widespread anxieties, anger and addictions, it's time to question the separation of the divine and temporal realms and seek to reunite them.

This is our work, but if we succeed it won't be our creation. Hello insisted that we can cooperate with God in this work, but not as equal partners. We can only do this work, paradoxically, while resting peacefully in God's sovereignty, confident of the efficacy of His revealed truth. Peace, Hello reminds us, is victory assured of itself.

Hello championed cooperative effort, discussion rather than suspicion and warm debate rather than cold silence. He unapologetically desired the conversion of opponents; loving-kindness could desire nothing less given the unifying eternal verities in which we are all embedded.

He wrote, "to cure an evil we must look it in the face." Hello looked various evils in the face, evils that are not at first glance so serious or obvious. Among them are indifference, envy, ignoring intransigent reality to embrace ephemeral ideas, and promoting mediocrity. He pointed to the cure: the values provided by the Creator of intransigent reality. The quality of this cure has been demonstrated by the saints. Always, humanity has the Church and her saints, the invisible God and "severe reality" calling us to choose life.

Hello's emphasised intellectual charity—loving-kindness to those who seek, struggling for enduring ideals. His clarifications in *Life, Science and Art* may help someone in their intellectual pilgrimage. Robust truth excited Hello. He didn't see transcendent truth as oppressive; instead it liberates us from confusion, slippery trends and manipulative disinformation.

People who topple the statues or denigrate the reputation of significant historical figures will find their activities reproved in *Envy*, and *The Mediocre Man*.

A post-modern pilgrim may benefit from Hello's frequent reminders that humans are receivers of truth, not its constructors. Our adventure in life, science and art—very broadly defined to include every human activity—is to discover and explore the truth we encounter. The misadventure of imagining that we create truths is not given to us; in fact, it is forbidden, condemned as pride's attempt at a misguided autonomy. We are finite creatures in a universe not of our making and if we refuse to submit to the physical and spiritual truths we discover, we will not prosper. Instead, we will die frustrated and unhappy.

We must act; choosing not to act is a form of action. We're often rightly concerned about the consequences of our actions, but we're less concerned about the consequences of inaction. We're alert to sins of commission, but we don't notice sins of omission. This shaded world is brought to the foreground in *Great Men, No Time!* and *Isolation and Solitude*. Our cautious timidity or indifference might leave someone floundering when we could've provided assistance.

Hello saw the human heart as a battlefield where ideas, appetites and emotions conflicted for supremacy. Spirits were battling too. Hello affirmed the reality of devils and angels, attendant to humans for evil or good. This is an unfashionable vision today, seeming almost ridiculous. But experience and the Church testify to the invisible influence upon us by powerful spiritual entities. Hello addressed this neglected aspect of our reality in *Unity, Death*, and *The Holy Angels*.

A pilgrim artist will find stimulating guidance in the chapters *Art, Contempt for Art*, and *The Ridiculous*. Hello considered Art an interweaving of Divine ideals, especially Beauty, with time and space. When Art is cheapened by ugliness or untruth it becomes tawdry and falsifying, and forgets the greatness of both Art and humanity. This forgetfulness, unfortunately, is widely evident in many forms of Western contemporary art.

Life, Science and Art is filled with hope. A chapter is dedicated to celebrating Hope. For Hello, Hope, together with Truth, Beauty, Peace, Justice and Life aren't impersonal abstractions. They're intrinsic attributes of a Person: God, for Whom all things are possible. Hello concluded his book with astonishing Hope for humanity:

> Every human act, even the most impotent, loses its impotence when united to the Self-Existent. God grants to us, and even commands us to accept, the glorious productiveness of an activity united to His own. We act in Him, and our very work is repose in Him.

Hello wrote whole words in CAPITALS for emphasis—I've substituted *italics*. In a few sentences I've italicised a word to make the meaning clear. The work is intact except for these minor changes.

Gary Furnell, Australia, 2024.

TRANSLATOR'S NOTE

Ernest Hello was born at Lorient in 1828. His father was a magistrate of high standing, a just and upright man, greatly respected in the neighbourhood. His mother, a clever, handsome, proud woman, possessing much nobility of character, was almost too careful of her delicate little son, and it seems probable that her excessive precautions did but aggravate his weak health. Ernest's childhood was passed on the old family estate of Keroman, near Lorient.

Beyond the wooded farms, where the peasants spoke Breton, lay the desolate *landes* and the grey sea. He loved these solitudes as a boy, and in manhood he returned to them to spend the best years of his life in strenuous literary work.

Hello was educated first at Rennes, then at the Lycee Louis le Grand, Paris. He studied for the Bar, but threw up his profession because his fellow-barristers decided in conference that it was quite permissible to defend an unjust cause. He could not, he felt, bear to be connected with a body of men, the majority of whom held such an opinion.

Long ago, as a mere child of four, Hello's uncompromising love of truth had manifested itself. He used to dress himself up in the most fantastic guise and play at being a tiger, crawling round the room on all fours and roaring horribly, while his mother fled from him in pretended alarm. When, however, he one day attempted by the same means to frighten away some rather dilatory callers, he was singularly unsuccessful. Instead of flying from the wild beast, the visitors were amused, and began to pet and caress him. " So, mother," said the child, when they were gone, "you were never really frightened at all! But how could you deceive me—a little boy like me?" Never, said Mme. Hello, did she forget the reproach in her child's voice.

So intransigent a nature would scarcely have been fitted in any case for the legal profession, yet his early training stood Hello in good stead when he turned his attention to journalism. For him, writing was a vocation; the writer's art, a sacred art. He was, indeed, endowed with that first and most indispensable gift of a writer — the gift of style; and this gift of his, together with all his other talents, he consecrated unreservedly to the service of Justice and Truth, as he understood them. "I have hungered and thirsted after Justice," he declares in the Preface to *Les Plateaux de la Balance*; "I have tried to do it, to think it, to speak it." Deeply religious, in Paris he had fallen under the influence of [Henri-Dominique] Lacordaire and [Alphonse] Gratry[1], the former of whom induced him to make a careful study of theology and Catholic philosophy.

In spite of his extremely delicate health, then, it was full of hope and energy that Hello, together with his friend Georges Seigneur, founded in 1859 a newspaper called *Le Croise*. Ably conducted, it was a success for a time, but it came to an end after two years in circumstances which led to a break with Seigneur. This was a bitter disappointment to Hello, whose ideal had been to found a paper which should be "the friend, the enlightened friend, of its readers" — which should "open its pages to all that was great and shut them to all that was petty." Yet, the world being what it is, one is not altogether surprised that a vessel sailed under these conditions should go under, more especially with so uncompromising a steersman at the helm as Hello.

Henceforth, Hello passed most of his time at his old country home of Keroman. He did not lessen his activity, but studied and wrote incessantly until his death in 1885. *L'Homme*, perhaps his most important work, was printed during the Siege of Paris in 1871. In it he treats of Life, Science, and Art, and shows how each, rightly understood, is a mirror that reflects the Face of God. *Physionomies de Saints*, a volume of charming little studies, appeared in 1875; *Paroles de Dieu*, a series of meditations on texts of Scripture, in 1878; *Contes Extraordinares* in 1879. *Les Plateaux de la Balance*, containing some criticism of doubtful value, but also the fine essay on Intellectual

---

[1] Henri-Dominique Lacordaire (1802-1861) and Alphonse Gratry (1805-1872) were French philosopher priests well-known in their era.

Charity, was published in 1880.

Hello was also a contributor to various periodicals, and some of his papers were collected after his death and published under the title of *Le Siècle: Les Homines et les Idees*. Another posthumous volume was, *Philosophic et Atheisme*.

Hello's life was one of continual suffering. The victim of some form of bone disease, which also affected his nerves, he probably owed thirty years of industrious life to the devoted care of the wife he had married in 1857. Zoe Berthier was twenty-four, and Ernest Hello eighteen, when they met for the first time. They became great friends, although for years Mademoiselle Berthier never contemplated marriage, telling her mother frankly: "Well, I'm not good-looking and I'm not rich. Probably I shall never marry. But one's life must be good for something, and I mean to be Ernest Hello's faithful and devoted friend. We two shall be old friends." When at length she became his wife, his mother confided to her that he had only six months to live. He lived thirty years more; and no view of Hello can be complete which does not take into consideration all he owed to the sensible, intelligent, and generous companion whom he was wont playfully to call Maman Zoe.

Ernest Hello may serve as an example of the heights to which journalism may rise in the hands of a man of genius inspired by high ideals. There were few men and subjects which came up for discussion in his day on which he did not write, always with striking originality, often with real insight. He was not afraid, as in *Les Plateaux de la Balance*, to traverse the intellectual world, pronouncing judgment, not only on his contemporaries, but also on the great names of Antiquity, with singular indifference to accepted views. Most Englishmen will dispute his verdict on Shakespeare, and there are many other cases in which we cannot accept his opinion, but he is always arresting and independent, and commands a respectful hearing.

He had formed a lofty estimate of the duties of criticism. "Criticism," he says, "should ennoble all the persons and things which it touches." And elsewhere he remarks, speaking of appreciation: "The happiness of a great artist is to admire another great artist."

It is not, however, as a critic, but as a religious and philosophical writer, that Ernest Hello claims our attention. He looked out into the modern world, where even good people often seem to have so inadequate a comprehension of the beliefs they profess, and, behind all the forces of confusion and disintegration, he perceived more clearly than most men the undoubted and imposing Unity of Truth. God is One: under all the phenomena of Time lies the Great Unity. All that is good and noble and generous in human life springs from Him; all that is true in Science rests on His Laws; Art, in its various forms, is a dim but infinitely sacred reflection of His Eternal Beauty. The humblest among us who strives to do God's Will and see things as they are — the saint, the scientist, the artist — all are looking at the same Face. There is no room here for clashing interests, for nervous dread of inconsistencies.

Hello was absolutely fearless in his deductions from first principles, and with spirit and confidence his voice rang out, reminding men that God is That Which is, and that outside God is nothing but darkness, disorder, negation, and the most utter boredom. He found it impossible, indeed, to indicate even approximately the horrible and appalling emptiness of all that is not God. "Truth is One," he proclaimed, "and religion, being true, can neither contradict nor embarrass Truth. . . . God is never in danger. Error is charged with its own destruction. . . . As Truth does not belong to us, we cannot concede one fraction of it."

His voice rang out; yet in his own day comparatively few heeded it. Hello was out of touch with his age; he disliked the century in which he lived, and spoke of its faults and errors with unmeasured scorn. He loved Justice and Truth with all the strength of his soul, and was firmly convinced of their ultimate triumph; but a strain of impatience in his nature made it difficult for him to wait, and he wanted the triumph to be immediate. He was not one to take comfort in the thought: "The truth is great, and shall prevail, when none cares whether it prevail or not."

Conscious of his genius, and ardently desirous of using it in the service of God, it was no small trial to Hello to be overlooked, and thus a touch of bitterness and personal disappointment has crept into his fine pages. There are moments when we almost feel that he is as angry with the sinner as with the sin — when we suspect that he classes most of his fellow-men among the mediocre, and despises them accordingly. We must not, however, forget to take into account in this connection the influence of continual ill-health on his outlook. It is by no means easy to preserve perfect intellectual calm under racking pain, and with nerves on edge. "The effect of my ill-health on my soul," he confessed once, in a moment of discouragement, "is simply hell. It makes me feel as if I were abandoned by God. It hinders me from working as a man of my temperament needs to work... It tempts me to doubt and to despair."

"He had the genius of a Saint, but not the sanctity," says his friend and critic Henri Lasserre, who at the same time bears an eloquent tribute to Hello's exceptional nobility of mind. His most striking characteristic, Lasserre considers, is loftiness of soul. "There is something of regal grandeur in Hello's genius; and those who aspire to intimacy with him must have in their own souls, and minds, and hearts, at least some touch of nobility."

How much there is in Ernest Hello that is winning as well as lofty! He who wrote so scathingly of mediocrity, wrote also with exceptional insight and feeling of charity, and practised in his own life, in a pre-eminent degree, that true charity which strives to satisfy the widely different needs of all with whom it comes in contact. Peasants loved him; beggars loved him — and, still more, he really seems to have loved them; animals loved him; the very swallows came to cheer him on his death-bed. With more than ordinary simplicity, it seemed to him quite natural to pray for the recovery of a poor lonely old woman's cat — her sole remaining companion. "Love makes men speak," he tells us. "Love enables them to understand what is said. Without love, men are nothing but deaf mutes."

We have shown that Hello's life was a life of study and intellectual activity. It was also a life of prayer. He prayed with his whole body and with his whole soul, often prostrate on the ground. The interior life of a man concerns none but himself and God, yet M. Joseph Serre has thought advisable in his biography to give us a few brief quotations from Hello's private prayers. Better than anything else, perhaps, they help us to a right understanding of him. He never presented a bold front to the world; his utterances were often drastic, sometimes scornful.

But the real Hello was not like that. We open the little manuscript book and turn the pages reverently. They speak for themselves, and any comment would be out of place. "Lord, I cannot carry Thy Cross except in the sunshine." "I am not a man; I am a child." "O my God, I can neither act, nor endure, nor wait! I am a prodigy of weakness." "Thou knowest that I am too weak to serve Thee by suffering. That is not my vocation. . . . Give me joy, then— joy!" "Lord, I am too weak to suffer and to die."

Genius is a gift of God, and, used conscientiously, it cannot fail in the long run to fulfil the end for which it was given. Ernest Hello died in 1885, and his voice seemed to pass away into silence. But Frenchmen, so susceptible to charm of form, could not long remain insensible to the grave beauty of a style which recalls the vibrating sentences of Pascal. Writing, as he largely did, for periodicals, Hello's work is often unequal, and he is inclined to repeat himself. He is at times prejudiced, even harsh, while some of his ideas are far-fetched. But he has written passages of rare strength and poetry; while there are others in which he speaks so vigorously, so abruptly, so trenchantly, as surely to rouse the most sleepy among us to be up and doing. Style, he ever held to be a man's most private property, the expression of his personality, his very self. And to his own canon of style he invariably adhered — namely, that a man should "live in accordance with Truth, think as he lives, and write as he thinks."

To-day Ernest Hello has come into his own, and his fellow-countrymen are reading his works with renewed interest and appreciation. *L'Homme* is now in its ninth edition, *Le Siecle* in its sixth. A new edition of *Paroles de Dieu* appeared in 1910; while *Physionomies de Saints* has been translated into English by Mrs. V. M. Crawford under the title of Studies in Saintship.

The present little book of extracts contains some of the most characteristic and suggestive passages in Hello's various works. In three or four instances a connecting clause has been added to link the thoughts together. It is not possible to render in a translation the force and beauty of much of Hello's prose; but even in the medium of another language his message has its value. He speaks to us from the grave, dwelling insistently on the Unity of Truth, the omnipresence of

God, the impossibility of getting on in any department of life without Him, the necessity for high ideals, and an intelligent grasp of first principles in the most ordinary details of human existence. He tells us — what indeed we know in theory, but are apt to forget in practice — that, after all, the Spiritual is the one great Reality. Barely hidden by our dream world lies the Real World of God.

"The angels keep their ancient places;
Turn but a stone, and start a wing!
'Tis ye, 'tis your estranged faces,
That miss the many-splendoured thing."

E.M.Walker. October 1912.

LIFE, SCIENCE, AND ART

I

THE ONE THING NECESSARY

THERE are circumstances that cause a man to retire into the interior of his own soul and think things over, and then the Utopias in which he has hitherto placed his confidence vanish. He feels himself in presence of severe reality — reality confronts him. In our day, however, good sense has become confused to such an extent that things have lost their names. Which is Utopia? Which is reality? Which are the dream things? Which are the things that belong to our waking hours?

One day a woman was preparing a meal for a Guest Who had come to rest for a while in her house[2].

"Master," she said, "my sister is not helping me." And the Guest replied: "Only one thing is necessary." Martha understood — in a certain measure, at least — the remark by which Our Lord established Mary's superiority. Martha understood, but the future generations, for whose instruction God also spoke, have never understood to this day.

All through the centuries to this very day, men have believed Christianity to be, as it were, a speciality — the speciality of those who fix their thoughts on another life, the speciality of mystics; and mysticism has been regarded as one of the forms assumed by dreams — worthy of a certain respect, perhaps, but assuredly useless.

And so the centuries, with their real, practical, pressing needs, have placed all their confidence in their own strength and skill. The result is that today the nations of the world no longer know how to surmount

---

[2]   This episode is recorded in Luke 10:38-42.

the innumerable difficulties of their situation. Yet they have what they wanted. They wanted to question matter, to probe it, to dominate it; they have done so.

And now, confronted by questions that concern the very life of nations, they cannot but see that *matter* does not solve them — that, on the contrary, it complicates them. Their discoveries contain no answer, their industry remains dumb. Weapons have been invented which give death; no instrument has been discovered which can give life. The advance of nations has raised a host of problems, just as the advance of armies raises clouds of dust; and in the obscure night which they have made around them, the nations have lost their way.

It was reserved for the age in which we live to spread out before man's eyes all the marvels of industry, to enthrone the conqueror in the midst of his conquests, and then to say to him: "You have placed your confidence in your inventions, and now you are going to die in the midst of them, to die on them, to die by them." In preceding centuries, humanity was embarrassed first by one set of details, then by another. Now it suffers from universal embarrassment. It is struggling in a labyrinth, and it is unable to set anything in order. However much trouble it takes, it always arrives at the same result — confusion.

Until now, man was tormented by various passions, such as love, hate, jealousy, avarice. Today, a society and a literature have sprung up which prove all too clearly that the trouble has struck at the very roots of the soul, changing even the old sources of disorder. Behind the passions that can be known and named, we see the return of another passion which had neither name nor existence during the Christian centuries, but which was called by the pagans *taedium vitae* [the tedium of life].

Now, to be weary of life is nothing else but to have an immense need of God.

The modern man, because he has succeeded in putting matter to all kinds of new uses, imagines that, among its thousand and one new forms, it will assume the form of a Saviour.

He treats as dreamers those who speak to him of faith, hope, charity, and adoration.

He thinks that He was not a practical man who said: "Seek ye first the kingdom of God and His justice, and all these things shall be added unto you."

This is why the modern man is at the end of his resources. He has abandoned his hold on the prey, and grasped at the shadow. Wise positivist though he deem himself, he does not yet even know that he has lost his foothold on the positive. He has made use of his success to bury himself in his Utopia. As his sleep has become deeper and deeper, his dream has become more and more unlike reality. And just as in his exterior life, man has turned night into day, day into night, so, in his interior life, he has tried to turn a dream into a reality, and a reality into a dream; only the nature of things has resisted the attempt, and the dream has remained a dream, the reality has remained a reality.

Jesus Christ remains what He always has been — the Cornerstone of this world, of all worlds. He remains the one universal necessity. Men do not want Him — they say that He is a dream; but He is the Reality, and nothing can ever get on without Him. Since matter, brought to bay and closely questioned, acknowledges its impotence, there is only one prudent thing left to do — to be converted.

The supreme necessity of the intellect, which is Justice and Truth, thus becomes the supreme necessity of life. The necessity for Jesus Christ has moved out of the region of Thought into the region of Fact. Christianity is no longer only the moral necessity of the world; it is also the material necessity. It is so urgent, this necessity, that one might well say it is the one remedy left to us. Palliatives are exhausted; truth alone is now practicable. There are no longer two different Saviours for this world and the next — there is only One for both; and it is He Who spoke nearly two thousand years ago to Martha and to Mary.

On land a sailor is sometimes blasphemous and drunken. But one day he embarks, and then, at the moment of farewell, a wife or a sister ties round his neck a medal of Our Lady, and when the wind rises, he remembers. The terrible voice of the tempest warns him of the limit set to the captain's skill, and busy though he is obeying orders, he finds time to lift his cap.

Thus, engaged as he is in the most material of occupations, he is reminded by the most material of all dangers of the most spiritual, the most mystical of all necessities — the necessity of prayer. And so the sailor, who perhaps a short time ago was drinking and swearing, is suddenly brought into complete harmony with a Carmelite monk praying a thousand miles away.

He has been led into the domain of the spiritual by the material violence of the raging elements, and it may be he will rise to great heights. Perhaps with one bound he will leave behind those who were once his teachers, for moments sometimes do the work of centuries. The howling of the wind is terrible, the ship very fragile, the sea very deep, Eternity something quite unknown.

Everything conspires to reveal to all of us today the same great spiritual necessity which the storm revealed to the sailor.

Unum est necessarium [the one necessity]. The one thing necessary, the one thing which men do not want, the thing which they declare antiquated and absurd, is that which all things are demanding as their principle, their bond of union, their very light. Without Christianity, everything will fall to pieces and we shall perish.

II

THE SPHINX

The Sphinx of Antiquity was a monster who propounded to all comers the enigma of Destiny. If they could not guess the meaning of the enigma, they were devoured by the monster. What could be more absurd? Yet what could be deeper, if men did but understand? Where is the truth, says Joseph de Maistre[3], which cannot be found in paganism?

There is a very singular word in human language. It is singular, because the thing it expresses seems beyond our control. Yet one trembles when one thinks of its importance to men. There is no recognized method of doing this thing, but no one can tell how great the regret may be of the man who fails to do it. The word I mean is this — to *guess*.

Life mingles people and things together: the good, the bad, the mediocre, the very good, the very bad — they all jostle against each other in the streets. Earth, which is grey, seems to throw a grey mantle over everything. Men resemble each other strongly, and we judge by appearances. Dress, it is true, makes an artificial dissimilarity, custom another, shyness another, dissimulation another, ignorance another.

Innumerable are the veils that hide realities from us. Men do not disclose their secrets; they conceal them under their various uniforms. A man looking down from his window at a crowded street would be dismayed if he reflected on the glorious or hideous realities passing before his eyes. They do not speak to him — they do not utter their names; they are disguised, veiled, profoundly hidden, and one is very like another, if appearance alone be consulted. But his dismay would increase, if this intelligent spectator of a silent crowd were to say to himself "My life, perhaps, depends on one of those men passing so

---

[3] Joseph de Maistre (1753-1821) Catholic philosopher, a teacher of conservative values.

close to me; perhaps some man I am waiting for, perhaps some man who is waiting for me, is there before my door. But there are so many people passing before my door! If he of whom I speak should be there, by what sign shall I recognize him?"

The history of Truth and the history of Error are alike full of meetings and events which seem the result of chance. The sight of all these things whose meaning it so behoves men to guess, and which yet they do not guess, drove Antiquity to the edge of a precipice, and the precipice claimed its victims. That precipice is called Fate.

The spectator I spoke of just now — he who watches the passers-by and asks himself vaguely if the man whom he seeks is among them — is on the high road to anxiety and despair if he be left to himself.

The private life of men; the public life of nations; the secret instincts of humanity; literature; history; the memories of the past; the needs of the present; the expectations of the future — everything warns man that he may need to guess, and yet there is no rule to enable him to guess *right*.

Hence the Sphinx.

If there were really such a thing as Fate, all questions would be insoluble, and the only answer to them all would be despair. But in general the questions which seem to call for hopeless answers have been incorrectly stated, and the hopeless answers are often as superficial as they appear to be profound.

Life is full of obscurities — happy he who can guess their meaning! Still, there is no acknowledged system of guessing right, no method which resembles a rule of arithmetic.

There is often in this world an unknown quantity to discover — an x, a big X, which defies the resources of algebra. The Sphinx of Antiquity desired that there should be no answer.

There *is* an answer, and we can kill the Sphinx. How can we guess?

A poor man comes along and craves hospitality.

Suppose he be the Angel of the Lord? But again, suppose he be an assassin? How can we guess? Must we make an effort of thought, an extraordinary act of the mind?

No, this is the secret: To guess is to love. Ask all those who have guessed how they did it. They loved — that was all.

The human intellect, left to itself, sets sail on an ocean of thoughts. It is confronted by the problem of Life, and if the compass is out of order, if the needle has lost the magnetic north, the intellect very easily arrives in practice at Doubt, in theory at a belief in Fate.

Love finds its way better. In practice it arrives at Light, in theory at Justice.

And here is an admirable truth: The recompense bestowed on the man who guesses and refused to the man who does not guess — the recompense which was a stumbling-block just now to the bewildered mind of the imaginary watcher at the window — this recompense, awarded or refused, is an example of supreme Justice, of a Justice far superior to the formal justice of men.

The man who guesses is rewarded, because he who guesses is he who loves. The man who fails to guess is not rewarded, because he who does not guess is he who does not love.

He who loves nobility, and who loves the poor and forsaken, will, when he meets the forsaken, recognize nobility if nobility be there.

He who encounters a man in need of something, will divine the need if he loves the man. And he who comes across the man of whom he stands in need, will recognize the benefactor he seeks, if he loves him well enough not to envy him his role — the role of giving and of pardoning.

III

INTELLECTUAL CHARITY

Whenever it is a question of material charity, people are to be found ready to help. Again, when it is a question of teaching the fundamental truths of religion to nations sunk in ignorance, heroes invariably come forward willing to devote themselves to this heroic task. But I want to speak now of a kind of charity which is often forgotten — intellectual charity.

Man has a thousand needs. He may be deemed as a creature of needs. He does not live by bread alone; he lives also by the Divine gift of speech. There are some men who have peculiar and exceptional needs — more than others, they need Light. There are other men who need ideas to come to them clothed in noble words. Not only the satisfaction of their intellect, but the very life of their soul (I might almost add, of their body) would seem to depend on Truth being presented to them in a form that they can desire, accept, assimilate. These men belong to the poor — a special class of poor; for they have one need more than most men, a need that is rarely satisfied. They are poor indeed, and the charity which cares for them is the rarest of all charities.

The Gospel speaks on many occasions of those who hunger and thirst, giving us plainly to understand that these expressions are used in their widest and most general sense. To hunger and thirst after Justice is numbered among the Beatitudes. But men seem curiously disposed to contract the meaning of the hunger and thirst which it is their duty to try and relieve. The more material a need is, the more pity it excites. On the other hand, the higher the type of need, the less compassion is felt for it. Many a man who would not dream of leaving another to die of hunger, in the material sense of the word, is not afraid to commit the same act in an intellectual sense.

Now, written speech may be a great charity, and its diffusion, whenever it is true and beautiful, is one of the acts of charity most suited to our time. In many souls, a hunger and thirst exists which can only be satisfied by printed words. Between these eager readers and the writer (who should also be eager) a current of sublime charity may be established, since all give and all receive. The reader gives an immense amount to the writer, and the writer himself does not know how much he receives from his reader. "To understand is to equal," says Raphael. No one can estimate too highly the importance of the journal[4] today — its rights, its duties, its responsibilities, the duties which we have towards it. For the journal distributes the bread of the intellect. It often penetrates where books do not penetrate. It educates the minds of men. Its influence is all the more profound, because it is for the most part unperceived. Its teaching is all the more effective, because it does not set out to teach. It is no pedant. It gives itself no professorial airs.

The Gospel has told us the very words with which the human race will be judged on the Last Day. We all think we understand these words, amazing though they be in their simplicity and their depth. But how many of us really understand them?

"I was hungry, and you gave Me to eat." "I was hungry, and you gave Me *not* to eat."

What strange, unheard of, unsuspected forms, will they not take, this hunger and thirst, on the Day of Judgment! What stupefaction will they not cause to men! A need which was quite overlooked, a need which was laughed at on earth, the need of some human soul which seemed nothing better than a whim to ill-natured and contemptuous eyes, will suddenly become of paramount importance. And Eternity — Eternity, with its two perspectives of endless joy and hopeless despair — may depend on the response which a man made to its appeal in the days when he lived on earth.

The hour will come when whoever has contributed, either positively or negatively, by act or by negligence, to the satisfaction or the non-satisfaction of the needs of a soul, will be astounded at the consequences of what may once have seemed to him an unimportant decision.

---

[4] Journal: more generally, print news media.

"Lord," he will say, "when did I see Thee thirsty, and not give Thee to drink?" And then he will remember, and be confounded. You will tell me, perhaps, that this is a very lofty way of considering the Press and its duties, and the duties which we owe to it.

Doubtless. It is lofty because it is true. Open the great books which are the foundations of Law and the sources of Light, and what is the first word which strikes your eyes? Charity.

More especially in the Gospels, charity glows like a flame before our eyes. The Good Samaritan, the Prodigal Son, the Lost Sheep, the Lost Piece of Money — there is no end to the instances. To come to the end of them, I should have to cite everything. But to cite everything in the Gospels which refers to charity, I should have to transcribe the whole of the four Evangelists, from the first line to the last. For even where charity is not mentioned by name, it is understood. The Gospels are for ever treating of charity, because they are for ever treating of God, and St. John tells us that God is Charity[5].

Charity is so deeply embedded in the world of thought that it is difficult even to imagine a system of religion that would not enjoin it. Erroneous doctrines twist its true meaning, and even change its nature; but still they adopt it, they preach it, they build upon it as on a necessary foundation. Say what men will, they always advocate charity. One can imagine the maddest, the most monstrous things, but one cannot so much as imagine an exhortation like the following:

> "My dear children, *do not* love one another. Let each of you think only of himself. Woe to him who loves his brother! Woe to him who remembers the poor!"

No! Such principles have never yet been taught, and they never will be. This, then, is certain: Charity is the foundation of every doctrine which has any reference to the human race. It would, therefore, seem evident that every man who is careful to listen to his conscience is, above all things, careful to practise charity. It is so in theory. It is not so in fact.

---

[5] Charity is the theological virtue of loving-kindness. Hello refers to I John 4:8.

In the life of many a man, attentive to his conscience and anxious not to wound it, charity, which occupies the first place in theory, occupies the last place in practice.

This phenomenon is so extraordinary that it seems to me necessary to state it very clearly, for to cure an evil we must first look it in the face.

Every man who strives to obey his conscience is very careful, and sometimes very scrupulous, on certain points of morality and conduct. But his care and his solicitude do not always extend to the practice of charity. I make an exception, of course, of all those who ought to be excepted: the Saints, whose lives form, as it were, a practical continuation of the Gospels, and those who seek with all their hearts to follow in the footsteps of the Saints, place charity before all things in their thoughts and in their lives. But I am not here speaking of Saints, or of those who in any degree resemble them. I am speaking of certain men who are striving to be conscientious.

And yet, you will tell me, there are a great many works of charity nowadays. Much is done for the poor.

Certainly, much is done for the *official* poor — for those who are officially labelled and assisted as poor. Those who occupy in the world the *position* of poor men are not forgotten.

But I am not speaking of this. I am not speaking of official works of charity. I am speaking of charity itself. I am speaking of charity as applied to all kinds of need, and I make no exception of the needs of the soul. I am speaking of that profound, interior charity, which asks itself in presence of another soul, another mind: "What are its needs? And what can I do to help to satisfy them?"

Here, for example, is a man who thinks, who meditates, who needs to give to others the fruits of his interior life. And other men need to receive these fruits. What can I do for the man who needs to give? What can I do for those others who need to receive what the first man is anxious to give? If I help the man who is in a position to give, I help at the same time the men who need to receive. The benefit is a double one.

The charity of which I speak is that intellectual and intelligent charity which springs from the soul and which seeks out the soul. Why is this sublime charity neglected by many conscientious people? It is because these conscientious people are afraid of doing evil, but they are not afraid of omitting to do good. They are afraid of sinning by act, but they are not afraid of sinning by omission.

We must love with all our heart, with all our soul, with all our mind. I do not know if such people love with all their heart and with all their soul, though I will admit that they do, if you like. But they do not love with all their mind. The mind is that which seeks, that which guesses, that which discerns. It is the sword of charity.

It is the mind that distinguishes good from evil; it is the mind that sees the difference between one man and another man. It is the mind that examines and explores, that probes the hidden depths of things. To love with all one's mind is to add justice to one's charity.

To love with all one's mind is to pardon superficial imperfections, and to attach oneself to the nobility concealed beneath them. To love with one's mind — with all one's mind — is to understand the needs of other minds, other souls. To love with all one's mind is to detect, wherever they exist, the hunger and thirst of the intellect, and to fly to their relief. To love with all one's mind is to go to the assistance of mind, wherever it lives, wherever it suffers.

"Blessed is he that understands the concerns of the needy and poor," says the Holy Scripture. Now, there are many kinds of poverty. I repeat of set purpose the sacred words: "I was hungry, and you gave Me not to eat." He loves with all his mind, who has been able to divine the needs of others.

IV

SOME CONSIDERATIONS ON CHARITY

We ought clearly to understand what is meant by *charity*. The more glorious a word, the more dangerous it may be. It is impossible to overstate the importance of language. Words are terrible in their complaisance. They lend themselves to any abuse, and make no protest.

It is just because charity is of all things most sublime, that the abuse of charity, and the employment of its name in a false sense, are exceptionally dangerous. *Optimi corruptio pessima*. [The best, corrupted, becomes the worst]. The grander the word, the more awful it is; and if the power which was intended to give life be directed against Truth, what service may not thereby be rendered to death?

Now, we use the word charity as a weapon against Light, every time when instead of crushing error we parley with it, under pretext of consideration for the feelings of others. We employ the word charity as a weapon against Light, every time we make it serve as an excuse for relaxing our execration of evil. As a general rule, men love to relax their efforts. There is something in the very act of faltering pleasing to human nature; and besides, the absence of any horror of error, evil, sin, and the devil, becomes a plausible excuse for the evil there is in us. To feel less detestation of evil in general is only perhaps a way of excusing ourselves for the particular evil we cherish in our own soul.

There is a verse in the Psalms to which little attention is paid. It is this: *You who love the Lord, hate evil*.[6] The day on which Evil entered the world, saw the birth of something irreconcilable. Charity — love of God — requires, supposes, implies, commands, a hatred of the enemy of God.

At the close of a long war, when each side is exhausted, kings have often been known to cede to each other such and such fortresses. They

---
[6] Psalm 97:10

are tired of fighting, and these concessions have the effect of silencing the cannon. But truths cannot be treated like fortresses. When it is a question of making peace in spirit and in truth, it is conversion we must have, and not compromise. Justice demands it, and it is not for us to tamper with justice.

In the relations between man and man, a reconciliation seems sometimes to take place, and yet there is no change in the heart of the offender, who thinks that a simple handshake will do instead of repentance and compunction for the wrong he has wrought. But it is not long before this false reconciliation reveals its true tendency, which is to lead inevitably to a second separation far wider than the first. The same holds good with regard to doctrines. Apparent peace, purchased by concession, is as contrary to charity as to justice, and opens out an abyss where before there was only a ditch. Charity must have Light, and Light avoids even the shadow of a compromise. All beauty implies completeness. Peace is perhaps, at bottom, victory sure of itself.

It is the crime of the age not to hate Evil, but to discuss terms of peace with it and make it proposals. There is only one proposal to make to it — that it should disappear.

V

GREAT MEN

There is on our earth a class of men deserving of quite especial charity and compassion, and yet we refuse them charity and compassion more often than we do others. The class I refer to consists of those whom we call great men.

Great men are poor men of a peculiar type, poorer than the other poor. A poor man is a man who is in need. The more needs a man has, the poorer he is. Birds hold no gilt-edged securities, but they are not poor, because they have no needs, or because they have only to spread their wings in order to find easily, and without the exercise of foresight, that which will satisfy their needs.

Man is the poorest of creatures. He is weighed down by needs. But the great man is so poor that in comparison all other men are rich. For the great man has, to begin with, all the needs of an ordinary man, and he is more conscious of them than anyone. And then he has other needs, at once higher and more imperative — needs which cry out more loudly, and which yet are much less often heard, because people do not understand. It is almost impossible for the great man to solicit help in these needs, for the public ear is closed to such cries for aid.

If Christopher Columbus had gone from door to door begging for ordinary bread — the bread which all men need, both great men and ordinary men — people would have listened to him more readily. But he begged for his own special bread: he needed ships with which to discover America. That was his bread. "Give us this day our daily bread." Ours! Not that of our neighbour, but *ours*, that which is specially necessary for us.

Now the bread which great men need is infinitely scarcer than the bread which ordinary men need. That is why great men are poor with an ordinary human poverty, because they have all the needs of man, and are also poor with their own special, exceptional, and peculiar poverty — a poverty which springs from the immense and unconquerable desires in virtue of which they are great men.

What, as a matter of fact, is the poor man who bears this terrible name — *great man?* I will try and answer this question.

When, in some solemn circumstances, a Sovereign sends an ambassador to another Sovereign, this ambassador is entrusted with a secret, and ought only to confide it to the Sovereign himself. When, in some solemn circumstances, God sends a messenger to humanity, this messenger is entrusted with a missive, a secret. Only, in this case, the secret is called mystery, and it is in virtue of this mystery that the great man is a great man.

Little men borrow all their importance from the actions which they accomplish. Without these actions, they would be absolutely nothing. They live by them, they exploit them. They beat the big drum and succeed in making some noise.

But they have no real substance. They are phantoms and will disappear. They always appear inferior to the place which they occupy and to the result which they obtain. They are crushed by their own works; and when these works are ended, their authors retire into their natural insignificance. The accident which brought them to the front bears them away again. Once the occasion which called them into being has passed by, these men exist no more.

The great man, on the contrary, is superior to his actions. The emotion caused by his name is more immortal than the accidents of history. This emotion is due to the mystery which surrounds him.

And that is why the great man is so difficult to judge. He acts in virtue of something we do not understand. Ordinary men may overwhelm him with a thousand reproaches, true or false, just or unjust. But they ought always to maintain with regard to him that attitude of respect demanded by the presence of the great Unknown.

Ordinary men — and above all, peculiarly little men — experience a certain charm, a certain pleasure, in attacking great men. There is much of the spirit of revenge mixed up with this pleasure.

These attacks meet with a certain success. But of one thing we may be sure: the success is due to the great man who is insulted. The curiosity men feel about him insures the notoriety of whoever attacks him. But this petty notoriety will be of short duration, and long after he who uttered the insults has passed into oblivion, the man, the great man, will stand before the world firmly rooted to his immortal rock, while the insignificant enemy will himself bear the scars of the very wounds he tried to inflict.

Not that I would forbid historical criticism seriously to examine the lives of great men. It is its right and its duty to call for their accounts, but it must be taken into consideration the elements of fraud and error characteristic of accounts, and it must also endeavour to rise to the height of the mystery it ventures to approach.

Generally, little men reproach the great man with not having done what they, little men, would have done in his place.

And it is true that the great man, had he acted as the little man would have done, would have avoided a thousand faults which he has perhaps committed.

As a great man, he has been subjected to a thousand defects. If he had done as the little men do, he would only have had one instead of a thousand. But the one defect would have been precisely this: he would have been no longer a great man.

If Christopher Columbus had been less obstinate, he would not have discovered America. Even at this distance of time, I seem to hear the words of advice he doubtless received:

> "But, my friend, be reasonable. Be like one of us. Why insist on standing out by yourself? Why not be like everybody else? Is that the example we gave you? Have your brothers, your cousins, your friends, your comrades, your uncles, your great-uncles, ever launched out into mid-ocean without knowing where they were going? Look to what lengths presumption can lead a man!"

You remember the celebrated mare who had every good quality except that of being alive, and only one single drawback — that of being dead. A great man who succeeded in being what little men desired him to be, would only have one drawback — that of being like them.

VI

NO TIME!

I HAVE no time!

He has no time!

We have no time!

It is the cry of our great cities. They are for ever conjugating the verb: *To have no time!* These four little words are very short, very quickly uttered. Yet how many things they imply! How many things they put a stop to altogether!

When I was a young man, literary discussion, intellectual discussion, roused and elevated the mind. We were full of eager thoughts, and our words were warm and enthusiastic.

What has become of enthusiasm? Today men are too busy; they are for the most part almost exclusively occupied with their business. Now, what is a man of business? The busy man, the modern man of business *par excellence*, is the man who has no time.

He is up to his neck in engagements; hopelessly entangled with innumerable acquaintances; harassed by a multitude of details, contradictions, unexpected misfortunes, difficulties; harassed also by the need of caution. On all sides are conflicting claims, complications. At every instant the crowd around him varies in costume and in appearance, but there is always a crowd — always a crowd followed by a crowd.

You accost a man, a friend, a brother. You are full of ideas and feelings which it is imperative that you should communicate to him in the interests of your common destiny. He needs your ideas, you need his, and the interchange of thought is really a necessity.

But all sorts of business matters are there clamouring for his attention. They watch for him, they throw themselves upon him, they load him with chains, they drag him away, bound hand and foot, to the cell where they stifle their victims.

And the words you were about to utter die away within you; they die away, not only on your lips, but also in your soul. They die away because the busy man who needs to hear your words, and whose words you need to hear, has no time to listen to you.

He has no time! What a terrible expression! We should do well to try and fathom the depths of its cruelty.

He has no time to work. He has no time to love. Should some important stranger cross his path — someone whom in his own highest interests it is most urgent he should know — he has not even time to perceive his presence. He has no time to act. For *to act* and *to bustle* are not two synonymous verbs. He bustles, he bustles, he bustles! He distributes to left and to right of him, here a word or two, there a shake of the hand, and his absent glance — absent because he is always in a hurry — never really rests upon anybody.

VII

ISOLATION AND SOLITUDE

Where is the land of exile? Every land which is not our true country is a land of exile. Our true country is the Light for which we were born. Exile is the night. Now, everything has its parody, and the greater the Light, the deeper the shadow which tries to counterfeit it.

The parody of our true home is a certain private dwelling — the black and isolated abode of egoism.

Sometimes man imagines that he will lose himself if he gives himself, and keep himself if he hides himself. But the contrary takes place with terrible exactitude. Do you know what is a man's most personal and private dwelling, what is beyond a doubt his own especial and exclusive retreat, the symbol and triumph of the complete man? It is called the grave. "Remember, man, that thou art dust, and unto dust thou shalt return," says the Church on Ash Wednesday.

The most private and undisturbed spot of all is certainly the grave. Then, if egoism were right, if he best kept himself pure and intact who shut himself up in the prison of his own being, sheltered from the fresh air and the outer world, the grave would be the one dwelling in which a man might hope to keep himself inviolate and integral. But admire what takes place! Egoism is so truly death that the grave hands over to decomposition, disorganization, and decay, the very man whom it shelters from air and life. It keeps what is confided to it, but keeps it for the worms that await their prey.

The grave is the man who shuts himself up in himself. You remember the words pronounced after those four historic days: "Lazarus, come forth!"

The same Voice speaks to every dead heart, and calls to it incessantly in the fullness of its love: "Come out of thyself! Come forth!"

The gift of self is the condition of life. The more a man opens his heart, the stronger he grows; the more he spends himself, the more concentrated he becomes; the more generous he is, the more master of himself; the wider the rays of his sympathies, the more glowing the centre.

But we must take care not to confuse isolation with solitude. Isolation is death, solitude is sometimes life. Isolation is privacy; but solitude, says Pere de Ravignan[7], is the country of the strong.

A selfish man of business, pushing his way through his enemies in the busy hurrying crowd of egoists, is not solitary, but he is isolated. The old anchorite of the desert lived in solitude, but no one was less isolated than he. He was in communion with humanity in its past, its present, and its future; for he was intimately united with Him, in and through Whom alone all beings are in communion.

Solitude favours union; for solitude, rooted in love and in order, elevates the soul, and it is always on the heights that union is prepared for and accomplished. Solitude is also a preparation for action, and often may be said to comprise action, just as silence prepares the way for speech, and often says more than words can say.

In the natural order, isolation weakens and solitude fortifies. An isolated man escapes many of the sorrows and burdens of life. A man capable of solitude first gathers together all that life can offer, and then spends it freely.

If we search for the very summit of solitude, our thoughts rest on the Cross that was raised on Calvary. And yet the Crucified Saviour reconciles all things, and draws all things to Himself: *If I am lifted up from the earth, I will draw all things unto Me.*[8]

---

[7]   Gustave Ravignan (1795-1858) French Jesuit writer.
[8]   John 12:32.

VIII

HOPE

Christianity places Hope among the virtues — among the theological virtues. It places it between Faith and Charity. If this sublime list of the things that are indispensable fell upon our ears for the first time — if the Word of Life spoke to us today for the first time this superhuman language — we should feel it to be superhuman. The command to hope can come from no other than God. But it is with the marvels of the catechism as with the marvels of the stars — familiarity breeds contempt, or, at least, indifference; and we have ceased to notice the extraordinary sublimity of the merciful command which forbids us to think ourselves lost.

It is not rare to hear men talk as though they thought that Christianity were a thing of the past — something already exhausted, its sap run dry; something which fears the future, and which, if it continues to exist at all when confronted by the future with all its greatness and science, can only exist by appealing for mercy. It is not rare to hear certain men talk as though they believed that Christianity stood in need of indulgence. They seem to think that the doctrines of the Council of Nicaea, the doctrines of St. John, the doctrines of St. Athanasius, must feel very timid in face of us moderns, in face of all the gas-lamps in our streets, and that it is a wise course for those who wish Christianity well, to plead in its favour some extenuating circumstances. In their minds, avowed or unavowed, is the thought that all that Eternal Truth can expect or hope for from us, is toleration.

By a strange self-deception, we take a great deal of pride in our own persons, and very little pride in our beliefs. It is time we became humble, for it is time we became proud. Let us abandon our souls to the radiant influence of Uncreated Light; let us become Its mirrors — Its burning mirrors, as it were — so that It is reflected back from us, and invades and penetrates those substances which have hitherto remained impenetrable and remote from it.

And, to attain this great end, let us all be at one — one with ourselves, one with each other. Hell strives with all its might to break the unity of those who recite the same Creed.

With one hand, it struggles to break the unity of Christian thought in the soul of the individual. It tries to persuade him that it is enough to be half a Christian, and that it is not necessary to be altogether and entirely Christian. It tries to persuade him that Christianity has no right to his whole soul; that there are certain reservations to be made, certain barriers to be erected, certain parts which must be set aside for the use of the spirit contrary to Christianity.

With the other hand, Hell struggles to break the unity of those who believe, by introducing into Christian society the great dissolvent of self-esteem. Hell stakes its highest on self-esteem, which is the principle of division and the cause of all divisions. It makes unparalleled efforts to establish coldness between Catholics; and he among us who accepts this proffered gift of coldness will indeed yield a valuable obedience to Hell. For coldness is in the moral order what paralysis is in the physical order.

In general, those who allow themselves to be divided lose the communion of love, and fall immediate victims to the spirit of darkness, who calumniates them one to the other, who deceives them, and who, above all, creates misunderstandings between them. A misunderstanding is one of the most effective practical methods of the spirit who works for division. Misunderstandings have for accomplices self-esteem and silence. There are hands made to clasp each other which never meet in a friendly clasp, because self-esteem and silence combine to paralyse them. There are men who would quickly love each other if once they were to speak to each other; for when they spoke, they would discover that their souls, united by the same intimate longings and Divine truths, had only been separated by phantoms and diabolic delusions.

What is it that we need in order to make us truly united? It is not, I think, the practical necessity for union which is lacking, nor is it the ideal beauty of love. Do you remember the day and the hour when we were commanded to love?

He Who spoke is called the Word. The Word lifted up His voice. And He Who listened was God the Father. In a very solemn moment, on the eve of the Crucifixion[9], Jesus raised His eyes to Heaven and said: "Father, the hour is come... And now glorify Thou Me, O Father, with Thyself, with the glory which I had, before the world was, with Thee."

These unfathomable words precede the prayer He utters for us. The Word has just spoken of Himself, now He is about to speak of us: "And not for them only do I pray, but for them also who through their word shall believe in Me: That they all may be one, as Thou, Father, in Me, and I in Thee: that they also may be one in Us..."

And, as if to reply to a foreseen objection, He gives them His Body, His Blood, His Soul, and His Divinity, to be the food of their souls — the same food for all, and a food which is Himself. To demonstrate unity, He institutes the Holy Eucharist.

I have entitled this chapter Hope, and yet it treats of charity. But, to justify my title, I will ask you to call to mind the concluding words of the verse we have just read: "That they also may be one in Us, that the world may believe that Thou hast sent Me."

Do you not now catch a glimpse of the reward of charity? Do you not hear, after the prayer, the promise?

Let us be one, in order that the world may believe that Jesus Christ was sent by God the Father. Do you not see how the future of the world is bound up with the charity which should unite us? Do you not see why I have called my chapter *Hope*?

Would you like to know the effect of charity on men?

"By this shall all men know that you are My disciples, if you have love one for another."

---

[9] The following is from John's Gospel.

God, Who is the Centre, draws near to those who draw near to each other; He draws away from those who hold aloof from each other. Only never let us imagine that the path to union is the path of surrender of doctrine. Let us not think that the war of ideas will ever be terminated by the abandonment of any truth. It is the whole Truth, adored in its full integrity, which alone can give us peace if we really desire it.

IX

UNITY

Death, in all its forms, is separation. Moral death separates man from Truth, which is his centre. Physical death separates the body from the soul. He who has a relish for death — its inventor, the devil — is he who is separated and who separates, he who does not love. Life, love, and unity, are inextricably connected, or, rather, they are one and the same thing.

Death, indifference, and separation, are three synonymous terms. What is it, then, which causes separation? What is the method of the arch-separator, Satan — Satan who does not love?

He tempts every man according to his character, his habits, his temperament, and thus only in certain exceptional natures does he arouse violent hate and opposition.

As a general rule, he knocks at the door which opens most easily of all — the door of indolence. Once this door is open, the ordinary man does not take the trouble to hate, for hate is tiring; but neither does he take the trouble to love, for love is a kind of industrious repose. Soon the man persuades himself that goodness is a negative thing; that, to be good, all he has to do is to do nothing at all; that only those are guilty who take the initiative with regard to evil, who put some passion and energy into their adherence.

The man who, influenced by the devil, sees things in this way — or rather does not see them at all — is deprived in a supreme degree of life and of love. He has fallen a victim to that fatal habit of mind, that contented blindness, which imagines itself wise and has no regrets; he suffers from a form of apathetic insanity, which lets Death slip in through an open door — Death with a friendly face, posing as a good-natured fellow who will not disturb the ways of the house, but will bring up the dinner at the proper hour, exact no sacrifice, and utter no alarming words. Such a man is supremely separated; all the more so because the separation has been accomplished peacefully, and he feels no uneasiness, terror, or remorse. Around him is the silence of the tomb, which is the parody of peace.

If ever this calm, unshaken, tranquil, and apparently unalterable state of death was the triumph of the devil, it is so in times like ours. We live in an age of war. The Spirit of Goodness and the Spirit of Evil confront each other on the battle-field of the world in the solemn attitude peculiar to decisive moments, and they are engaged in questioning, numbering, and marshalling their soldiers. They question them, they number them, they marshal them; but the Spirit of Goodness rouses them and excites them to action, while the Spirit of Evil lulls them to sleep.

The Good Spirit says: "Let the dead bury their dead. Arise! Take up your bed, and walk."

The Evil Spirit says: "You had better rest. What good would you do in the battle? There will be plenty of others to fight. You who are wise had better keep quiet. Evil has always existed, and always will exist in the same proportions. The madmen who insist on fighting it, gain nothing, and have no time to rest. You who are wise would do well to live and let live, and not to make war on anything. It is impossible to enlighten men. Why, then, attempt it? Live on terms of peace with the opinions you do not share. Are they not all equally legitimate?"

Thus speaks the devil; and hence forth the man, pledged to disunion, invokes the authority of the very disunion whose author and accomplice he is, to uphold him in not working for union. He first renders unity impossible for himself, and then declares it impossible for everybody. He *will* not, and so he declares that he *can*not; he creates in himself an impossibility, and then proceeds to point it out. Sometimes he maintains that a vague kind of unity of mind and spirit is quite sufficient. Of what good, he then says, are definite dogmas? Sometimes he confesses that there is no unity outside Catholicism. But, in either case, he gives up the hope of seeing unity revive in himself and others.

He gives up! This is the important word! This is the devil's word!

This is the point I wish to impress upon you. It is the word that Satan whispered in the ear of Judas. It is the suicide's word, an expression connoting *ennui*, despair, Hell. God never gives up! The devil always gives up, even when he pretends to go on acting. The man who gives up accomplishes nothing, and is only a hindrance. The man who does not give up can move mountains.

What man has the right to utter the word *impossible*, since God has promised to be with us and to help? Let those unite together, then, who have not given up, and let them unite in hope — in a living, ardent, active, fruitful hope. In the hour of battle, the soldier does not require that his comrade should be perfect; he does not try to rake up some grievance against him: he knows that he is his comrade, that they are fighting side by side, that they are sons of the same country, and he does not stop to think of anything else.

If ever a man and a Christian should forget little personal divisions, it is surely on the field of battle. *Unity and Hope* — that is the motto of victory. When we declare the progress of Truth and the triumph of Beauty to be impossible, we thereby render them so. We cease to hope for them, because we have ceased to strive for them. Men only strive for what they hope to get. Let us dare to hope for victory, and it is possible. Let us resolve to win it, and it is ours. It is ours, but on this condition: That all who dare to hope should stretch out a helping hand to those who dare to fight. There is another condition; it is that each one of us should realize the necessity of lending his personal aid to all who hope and all who fight, and that he should not expect others to pay his share of the tribute. What would become of a world in which everyone counted on others to do things, and so no one did anything at all?

X

THE SPIRIT OF CONTRADICTION

As long as I can remember, I have noticed that men are continually disputing together, and doubtless you too have noticed it. Universal contradiction is a universal fact. Division covers the earth. It is not between enemies that we find the deepest division; it is between friends. Where union seems to exist, there division exists, all the more radical and intimate because of the apparent union. I do not enlarge upon this fact; I simply state it without discussing it. The intellectual condition of the human race is a masterpiece of division. Yet I am sure that if I could contemplate men as they really are in the depths of their souls, solitary and recollected, they would not look at such a distance from each other, so separated, so divided, as they do when I see them in the midst of the turmoil of life.

Why do they appear to be greater enemies than they really are? They are made for union, and division is their misfortune. Why do they add to their misfortune, the misfortune of being divided?

The question is of immense importance, of universal importance. The fact is, there is in the world a monster called the Spirit of Contradiction.

Everything I consider in the world, I can consider under several aspects, and so can you.

Paul sees a thing on a certain side; it looks to him white.

Peter sees the same thing on the other side; it looks to him black.

Both are right, both are wrong, for the thing is white on one side and black on the other.

"It is white!" cries Paul.

"It is black!" cries Peter.

And behold two enemies!

The Spirit of Contradiction shuts their eyes and embitters their hearts, and blinds and separates their souls.

The whiter the thing looks to Paul, the blacker it looks to Peter; and Peter sees it horribly black because Paul sees it excessively white. Their eyes, instead of coming to each other's aid, are aflame with irritation.

They were two intelligent men, made to understand each other. Now they are two enemies, stupidly obstinate, stupidly blind, all because the Serpent of Contradiction has raised his head between them.

The thing is so simple that its simplicity hides its importance. If Peter is to show Paul to any good purpose the black side which he sees, he must first perceive as clearly as Paul the white side which Paul sees, and he must tell him so. If he does not frankly tell him so, each will hopelessly entrench himself behind his individual point of view.

This is why kindness of heart has such an immense role to play in the reconciliation of minds. If you are irritated with your enemy, who perhaps, after all, is your friend, you will never convince him.

Peter imagines that if he were to grant Paul all that he can grant consistent with truthfulness, Paul would take advantage of his avowal and use it against him. But the absolute contrary is the case. Paul will see what Peter sees, when Peter has seen what Paul sees and candidly acknowledged it.

I was but a child when I was led into forming erroneous opinions about many things, just because I was so often contradicted. And ever since that time I have seen clearly that the Spirit of Contradiction is Satan himself, the father of all lies.

Father Faber[10] holds that we shall never convince a man unless we first prove to him that we have thoroughly grasped all his objections and

---

[10] Frederick William Faber (1814-1863), English theologian who converted from Anglicanism to Catholicism and became a priest.

entered into his point of view. Nothing is more true.

Father Faber also says that there is one thing in the world which can never, in any case, do any good. This unique thing is sarcasm.

You have an antagonist. Laugh at his point of view: he will never see yours. Never! You have shut off from this man the sources of Life. Father Faber further says that if a man were suddenly to begin to look with friendship on all other men, and to put a *favourable* construction on their conduct, this man would find existence as completely altered as if he had been transported to another planet.

In education, in discussion, in science, in criticism, in public life, in private life — everywhere, everywhere, the same fact may be observed: the earth is covered with ruins, and it is the Spirit of *Contradiction* that has caused them.

St. Mary Magdalene of Pazzi[11] adopted the following for her rule of life: Never refuse anybody anything, unless it be an absolute impossibility to grant it.

Here is the spirit which is the exact opposite to the Spirit of Contradiction.

The experience of centuries teaches us that men need consoling first, instructing afterwards. They do not understand the instruction until they have received the consolation. The Spirit of Contradiction violates this law. It *will* begin by speaking of the cause of irritation; it puts the obstacle in the foreground. It sets out by a reproach. It irritates before it tries to pacify. That is why its teaching is sterile and fatal, even were it a hundred times in the right.

Begin with argument, and all will be sterile.

Begin with love, and all will be fertile.

The Spirit of Contradiction resides in the soul and gives the man who

---

[11] Mary Magdalene de' Pazzi (1566-1607) Italian Carmelite nun and mystic, patron saint of the sick.

speaks a certain *tone*. If tone is so important in speech, it is because the tone indicates the attitude of mind. The tone is more important than the words used.

Let us suppose that Father Faber's hypothesis has been realized, and that this very day men have adopted kindness as the principle of all their actions.

To-morrow we shall be living on another planet.

But, you will tell me, differences of opinion will still exist.

I do not say that they will all vanish. But we shall be astounded if we one day see the small proportions to which they are reduced.

If the huge misunderstanding created by the Spirit of Contradiction were to disappear, we should be amazed to see to what a great extent the union of intellects would follow the union of hearts.

XI

APPEARANCE AND REALITY

I want the reader to lend himself to a supposition. Let us suppose that we have to do with a stranger from another planet, someone quite ignorant of the ways of our world, and that we are showing him some of the sights which meet our eyes down here.

We take him first to a battle-field. What a horrible tumult! The whistling of the shells, followed by their explosion! The deadly combat! The wounded, the dying! All that bloody confusion which Chateaubriand called *la cohne de la mort*.

The stranger turns to us and says: "I did not know what Hate was, but now I know. I am horrified. I am appalled. Hate is, then, the invention of men. Not deeming themselves sufficiently mortal, they have summoned Hate to the aid of Death."

To calm our traveller and to vary his course of instruction, we will bring another picture before his eyes. We will take him to a reception in high society. Instead of cries of pain and bursting shells, he will meet with nothing but greetings and smiles. For here civilization reigns, here it flourishes, here the art of polite speech is found in perfection.

There are neither men nor women in the elegant apartments; there are only gentlemen and ladies. The words exchanged breathe the most admirable courtesy. Nobody emphasizes his remarks unduly. Nobody utters a sharp word. The opinions expressed are never far from the golden mean. Nobody is very religious: that would be going a little far. Nobody is very irreligious: that, too, would be going a little far. Nobody is very authoritative: that would be disagreeable. Nobody is very revolutionary: that might give offence.

Nobody owns to any positive faith: that would be a little old-fashioned. But each is ready to give what protection he can to old beliefs, for their destruction among the lower classes would not be without drawbacks, especially their complete destruction — for we must have nothing quite complete. Not that it is really desirable that the people should preserve a definite and living faith. By no means! Still, one would wish them to retain some vestiges of trust in Providence, some vestiges of fear. It is rather a good thing when the poor hope for certain rewards in another life and dread certain punishments. It helps them to support the miseries of this world, and in all things prudence is necessary.

Our stranger begins to feel reconciled to men. How kind and amiable they are! How moderate! We are far enough away from the battle-field now. We call his attention to a group of gentlemen on his right, and to a group of ladies on his left. The gentlemen are talking politics and literature. Two in particular are arguing together. We do not hear all they say, we stand at a little distance looking and listening, but we gather that they are talking of modern writers. They blame severely those people of strict views who believe all they feel bound to believe. "Sometimes," says one gentleman, "it may be necessary generously to sacrifice one's own convictions for the sake of others, and the interests of Truth for the sake of harmony." This remark is almost unanimously approved. Still, someone does venture to contradict and to say: "Can there be any harmony without Truth?"

The shadow of a smile flits over the faces of the listeners, and in certain eyes there is a cold flash which resembles steel. We now turn to the group of ladies. Surely the flowers, the diamonds, the radiant and smiling faces, exclude any idea of hostility or revenge? A dexterous wave of the fan conveys here a greeting, there a sign; the most exquisite politeness presides over every movement. Now and again, the slightest of gestures emphasizes certain words. But how could anyone imagine that the term "my dear," uttered in a certain tone of voice, should be meant as an impertinence? It would be impossible to think that, would it not? Yet these elegant women survey each other with a cursory glance, and guess, imagine they guess, or else unconsciously reveal a thousand secrets. But without a long and terrible experience of the world and its ways, how could one distrust a basket of flowers?

If a dart should pierce and chill the heart, would it be likely to have first concealed itself in a basket of flowers? No! Such a suspicion will never enter the noble mind of our companion. The stranger from a distant sphere who has just been appalled by the horrors of the battle-field, is actually reassured by the pleasing picture of our kindly civilization. He believes that, whereas a short time ago he was contemplating hate, the charms of kindness are now being unfolded before his eyes.

Well, listen! If I were really charged with his education, if it were my duty to initiate him into terrestrial matters, I should say:

"You are making a radical mistake. The dust of the battle-field contains not an atom of hate. The men who are now killing each other will be quite ready presently to help and assist each other. After having risked their lives in an attempt to kill others, they will soon perhaps be risking them with the contrary intention of saving the lives of their enemies. The word *enemy* has in this connection a special and mysterious sense. The enemy is the man who happens to be confronting you. In fighting him, you obey a decree which you do not understand; you obey a feeling of fury which is not really yours, which springs from something higher than your personal sentiments."

"But," interrupts the stranger, "where is hate to be found if it is not to be found in death?"

Where is hate to be found? Perhaps in that very drawing-room where just now you were admiring the suavity and elegance of our social intercourse. It lies, perhaps, in those smiles, those artifices, those reticences, and above all, in those silences. "You are angry, therefore you are in the wrong," said one of the Ancients. The remark is as false as it is celebrated. I should much prefer to say, "You are angry, therefore you love." A man who is liable to grow angry is almost always a man of deep affections. His may be "the anger of love," to quote Joseph de Maistre.

The man who gets heated in argument, who pursues his adversary with accusations, who wishes at all costs to carry the citadel by storm, to convert, to persuade, is a man full of affection. The apparent violence he displays with regard to you, is really only an ardent desire to unite himself to you, and to bear you away with him to the regions of peace and victory. If you repulse him absolutely, he will end by being silent, and then, indeed, he will love no longer. In discussions among educated people, the man who tends to get heated is accused of giving way to hate: he is really the man who loves.

He who can manage to maintain a perfect moderation, who never allows a word to escape him beyond what is dictated by prudence and calculation, he whose words and demeanour remain irreproachable, is often he who does not love. The other man gave himself to others; this man reserves himself, and seems amiable because he is indifferent. Hate is not a violence; it is a reticence. It is not ardent; it is cold. It is a negative quantity. It is not a transport of passion, but a holding aloof.

He who loves is moved to speak, and so is he who believes. "I have believed, therefore have I spoken." He who has ceased to love is silent. The life that is based on hate is based on silence. Certain almost imperceptible shades of expression and gesture serve, as it were, to accentuate the silence; they indicate the degree below zero to which the frozen temperature of separation has fallen. For this is the true name of hate: it is neither pursuit nor reproach nor fury — it is separation.

XII

INDIFFERENCE

Many people who know nothing about it, reproach Truth with being intolerant. This needs explanation. One would say, to listen to them, that Truth and Error are two beings with equal rights; two queens, both legitimate, who should live in peace, each in her own kingdom; two deities, who divide between them the allegiance of the world, without one having the right to seize the domains of the other. And from this mode of thought springs indifference, which is the triumph of Satan. Hate pleases him, but hate is not enough; he must have indifference.

Indifference is a unique kind of hate, a cold and lasting hate which hides itself from others — sometimes even from itself — behind an air of tolerance. For indifference is never real. It is hate combined with falsehood.

To continue to pour forth day after day a torrent of fierce invective against Truth, men would require a decision of character which they do not possess.

Accordingly, the line which they take is to take no particular line. And yet a noisy hate is much more easily explained, once original sin is granted, than a silent hate. What astonishes me is not to hear some blasphemy on the lips of a man. Original sin is there; free will is there; blasphemy has its explanation. What plunges me in a stupefaction absolutely beyond expression is neutrality.

It is a question of the future of the human race, and of the eternal future of everything in the universe possessing intelligence and freedom. It is certainly and of necessity a question of you yourself, as, indeed, of every person and everything. Then, unless you are not interested in yourself, nor in anybody nor anything, it is certainly and of necessity a question of an interest most sacred to you. If you are alive at all, rouse up the life in you. Take your soul, and rush into the thick of the fight.

Take your wishes, your thoughts, your prayers, your love. Catch up any weapon which you can possibly wield, and throw yourself body and soul into the struggle where everything is at stake.

Placed on the battle-field between the fire of those who love and the fire of those who hate, you must lend your aid to one or the other. Make no mistake about it. The appeal is not to men in general, it is to you in particular; for all the moral, mental, physical, and material gifts at your disposal are so many weapons which God has placed in your hands, with liberty to use them for or against Him. You must fight; you are forced to fight. You can only choose on which side.

Jesus Christ, when He came into this world, asked men for everything He needed, for He chose to be poorer than the poorest among them. He asked for a place in which to be born: it was refused Him. The inns were full; a stable door was the only one open. He asked for a place in which to dwell: it was refused Him. The Son of man had not where to lay His head. And when it came to His death, He had not six feet of ground in which to lie. Earth rejected Him, and He hung between earth and sky on a Cross.

Now, He Who asked then, asks still. He asks for a place in which to be born. The people who filled the inns, and who would not put themselves out, but sent Jesus away to be born between an ox and an ass, are an admirable figure of those men who are forever sacrificing themselves and their future to inexpressibly dull and empty trifles.

Of all the mad ideas inspired by the devil, this is that most worthy of him: Truth is dull. Truth *dull*! but it is the possession of Truth which constitutes beatitude. Truth *tedious*! but Truth is the foundation of ecstatic happiness. All the splendours we perceive are but feeble symbols of Truth. Even its distant rays cause an indescribable rapture.

The human soul is made for the Divine pastures, not only in Eternity but in Time. There are not two sources of happiness. There is only One; but It will never run dry, and all may drink from It. Are you in love with *ennui*? It is towards the non-existent that you must attempt to look. But are you in love with life, in love with happiness, in love with Love? Then turn to Him Who Is.

Satan is the Prince of *Ennui*, of despair, of unhappiness.

God is the Master of Joy. Let the indifferent examine themselves, then, and stand condemned.

XIII

LIGHT AND THE PEOPLE

Among the most fatal of the errors that prey upon humanity, I desire to point out one which does untold harm. This error is all the more fatal because it often takes possession of well-intentioned people, with the result that it breaks the weapons in their hands. The error I allude to is as follows:

Many a man, confronted by the loftiest principles of metaphysics, argues in this fashion:

"What does it all matter? Transcendental theories, whether false or true, never reach the masses. I wish to do what is right, and I find myself surrounded by men who have neither read the great philosophers of Truth nor the great philosophers of Error. The theories of philosophers are a kind of ingenious mental gymnastics, but they exert no influence on the world. Let us have practical things."

In the opinion of the man in the street, principles are not practical things.

The ordinary man believes that the great principles of Eternity are absolutely useless to the happiness of his daily life. And so men say to each other:

"What does such or such theological question matter to my practical life? What difference could be made to my practical life by such or such a definition of the Church with a purely metaphysical bearing?"

You want to know what it matters? Well, you might as well say: "What does it matter to me whether we have Saints or whether we have egoists?"

A thief takes your purse. You have no time to think of the great principles of Eternity. You merely run to the police-station.

You are perfectly right to go to the police-station. But the root of the trouble is that certain eternal truths have been forgotten.

Secondary principles have only a limited application. Primary truths are capable of universal application.

The more fundamental a truth, the more practical it is. The more *essential* it is, the more useful it is in face of what is *accidental*. The more terrible the accidents, the more necessary it is to appeal to the most essential, the most lofty, and the most transcendental truths.

Today, as in the time of David, help comes from the mountains[12]. I beg all who wish to do what is right to listen to what I am going to say. Always and everywhere, the principles of the loftiest metaphysics govern the masses most ignorant of metaphysics — not directly, it is true, but indirectly. The private life of man, in its humblest details, is the translation into action of the metaphysics he has adopted; and private life today is all the worse because an erroneous metaphysics has been accepted so generally and for so long. Every man who acts, acts well or ill in obedience to some abstruse metaphysical theory, of which nearly always he knows nothing, but which others know for him.

You who elbow the passers-by in the street and who say, "What does it matter?" in face of the sublime truths which you deem abstract, you resemble a baker turning the loaves in the interior of his oven, and saying of the light, "What does it matter to me?" To listen to men, one would suppose that God had ordained no connection between the rays of the sun and the bread which they eat. They do not realize how the grain ripens. They forget the very light which nourishes them.

In all ages the blind have said: "What does it matter as regards practical life to know if the Holy Ghost proceeds from the Father and the Son or not?" Look at the earth: compare the regions that affirm with the

---

12 A reference to Psalm 121:1,2.

regions that deny, and tell me which countries produce Saints. Think of the close and mysterious relations between light and food. I spoke just now of sunshine and bread. Certainly the light and warmth that stream down upon our fields blessed with a golden harvest, in no way resemble a piece of bread. If men were as ignorant of the physical order of things as they sometimes are of the moral order, they would say with reference to bread: "What does light matter to us? What does warmth matter to us?" And yet, what is bread, except a ray of sunshine imprisoned in matter and kneaded into dough by the labour of man?

The peasant who cannot read, but who, as he works in the fields, pauses a moment and lifts his cap when the Angelus rings, is nourished by Light and has need of God.

No one can grasp in whole and in detail the action of Light on the world; no one can know what good a true word will do, what harm a false word will do. No one can follow the flight of his words through space and mark their every curve. No one can set what limits he will to the distant consequences of a truth, the distant consequences of an error. No man when he attacks inviolable orthodoxy, even on the point which appears to him the most remote from practical life, can possibly foresee what act, in the order of facts, his negation will one day produce.

XIV

THE AGE AND THE AGES

One of the most despicable forms of Error is fashion, and yet clothing ought to be a thing of beauty. What is fashion, except that particular form of clothing which the period forces a man to wear? A fashion is ridiculous once it is out of date; yet, if clothing were what it might be, it would be possible to alter its form today without making the form of yesterday look ridiculous. Yesterday's fashion is ridiculous to day because it was modelled on the spirit of the age; and it appears in all its ugliness as soon as it ceases to be supported by purely accidental, external, and transitory conditions.

Now let us admit the following supposition. Suppose somebody today were to invent a religion.

The difficulties would be innumerable. I will not attempt to mention even the more important ones, for I should never have time. But I will take a minor detail — the distinctive dress of its priests. They would have a distinctive dress, I suppose, and I challenge you to imagine one which you could look at, or even think of, without laughing. And yet, be you who you may, have you ever felt inclined to laugh at the sight of a Catholic cassock, even a torn one? Have you ever been moved to exclaim, "How old-fashioned!" No. For you were outside the dominions of fashion. The man in a cassock may have seemed to you a reproach, but not an anachronism, for he did not belong to the age.

The Prince of Evil is called the Prince of this World. He is the Prince of the Age, but the Church declares that God shall reign throughout all ages. In the Garden of Olives, Our Lord said to those who came to seize Him: "This is your hour and the power of darkness."

Your hour! Evil was to be permitted the triumph of an hour. But to His friends, Our Lord said: "I am with you all days, even to the consummation of the world."

An hour! All days — all ages! How much may be learnt from this contrast! And even during the hour accorded to the power of darkness, Jesus promised the Good Thief that Paradise where glory endures *in aeternum ei ultra* [forever and beyond].

The property of Error is to have only a moment to live, as the property of Truth is to have all Eternity before it. Thus, one is patient, the other is hurried.

The Catholic Church dominates the ages. She speaks of Eternity with singular familiarity. Nations and centuries, Time, Space, all you that change, all you that pass, listen and look.

Look how Truth, sure of itself, spreads among all nations and through all ages, without any stumbling or inconsistency. See how sure it is, how it never contradicts itself. See how it is exempt from the germ of death. See how it can stretch forward in all directions and yet no part of it ever clash with any other part.

God is never in danger: Error is charged with its own destruction. There was an age — the age of the French Revolution — when men conceived the project of doing away with Christianity. The absurd attempt to replace God by the Goddess of Reason very soon put an end to that project. It killed rationalism, the philosophy of the eighteenth century, and since then the devil has changed his tactics. He no longer suggests that men should do without Christianity, but he advises them to modify it. He no longer represents Christianity as a shameful absurdity, but he represents it as an excellent human doctrine; he is ready to admit that it is the best possible of things, provided only that it be a human thing. He is willing to praise Jesus Christ with the utmost enthusiasm, provided that men will only agree that Jesus Christ is not God.

Now, to obtain this result, to arrive at a purely human Christianity, do you know what is the best method? It is to separate morality from dogma, and to say to men: "The morality of the Gospels is sublime. Confine yourselves to the morality. At bottom, all nations have the same morality; they only differ with regard to particular dogmas. Morality unites men; dogma divides them. Let us, on our side, concede the superiority of Christianity; then, if only Christianity will make us a few concessions, we shall all be of one mind."

If the devil could only obtain this, he would have obtained everything. But it has been written: *Non praevalebunt* [they will not prevail].

As Truth does not belong to us, we cannot concede one fraction of it.

The devil loves to suggest that dogma is the obstacle to peace, and that peace would soon ensue if men would agree to reduce Christianity to the level of a course of lectures on morality.

I am not going to insist here on the fundamental absurdity of sacrificing a dogma, of denying a truth, from motives of expediency. To listen to some men, one might suppose that Truth was our property, and that we could give it away when we liked. One might suppose — but there is no end to the absurdities one might suppose. Let us look at the facts.

Catholicism and Protestantism have followed two different courses.

Catholicism, like God, has remained rooted in immutable Truth, and, like Him, it has remained rooted in immutable Unity. It enjoys peace, because it has only sought it on the terms laid down by God. Protestantism, because it has fallen from Truth, has fallen from Unity; it has been willing to betray Truth for the sake of peace, and so it has met with war.

Catholicism, because it has sacrificed no dogma, has been able to rear, maintain, and propagate that chosen race of men which carries morality to the height of sanctity; while Protestantism, though for ever talking of morality, has no Saints, because it has been faithless to dogma. Does it know this? Does it understand it? Does it regret what it has lost? I think not. For it has lost even the idea of sanctity, even the memory of it.

Saints! The very name is so extraordinary that I do not know how anyone can pronounce it without being forced to reflect. How can you help seeing the distance, how can you help seeing the abyss, between a Saint and an honest man — an honest, good man, even a pious man? And if you see the abyss, how is it that you do not look at it carefully?

And if you really look at it, what can you be doing not to understand?

If you have ever been tempted to think that by abandoning certain dogmas or exterior observances, men would be better able to concentrate themselves on the practical side of life, on doing good and on being charitable — if, like many others, you have ever been tempted to think this, close your History of the Age and open the History of the Ages. Where are the Saints? Where do you find the recruits of the triumphant army, the army of God? Among the deserters of dogma, or among its defenders?

Represent to yourself a man who denies a dogma — that dogma of all others which seems to you the most useless to morality — and try to give that man the name of *Saint*. I defy you to do it. You cannot.

O true descendants of the *word made flesh*, torches that light up the world with the glory of God, wonderful flowers! Where are the lands that have the secret of producing you? Whence do you come? Where do you flourish? Stars of the night, tell me in what country the traveller may find you? Which country is your country?

Your country is the Church, and the traveller will find you in the lands where the Blessed Virgin has her altars.

XV

CONTEMPLATIVES AND LUNATICS

The world reproaches the Saints with being mad, and regards contemplation as a form of hysteria. The Saints do not contradict it; and Christianity, which speaks of the folly of the Cross, is by no means astonished at such language. Only it must be clearly understood what is meant, and the world understands nothing.

One of the characteristics of madness is caprice. Each madman has his own special delusion, which does not resemble that of his neighbour. Madness is eminently subject to any caprice of the imagination; it loses sight of all general and restraining principles, and abandons itself to any individual, momentary, and unhealthy impulse which has taken the place of health and sanity. These impulses are of infinite variety, and every lunatic has his own peculiar one. The man who should suggest to the inmates of a lunatic asylum — still more, to the inmates of all the lunatic asylums in the world — to agree together and embrace a common form of lunacy, a similar and self-same delusion, would, indeed, be very mad himself.

Now, the peculiar characteristic of contemplative theology is unity of faith, orthodoxy.

Search the histories of Catholic contemplatives from end to end. You will find learned and ignorant people — men, women, nuns, wives, virgins, scholars, peasant women — and, together with the most perfect diversity of nature, character, and conditions, you will find the most perfect unity of doctrine. You will find, then, the very thing which is absolutely, radically, and necessarily incompatible with madness, and I do not see how any man of good faith can possibly escape from the irresistible evidence of this incompatibility.

Again, another characteristic of sanctity is prudence.

Consult any one of those Saints whom the world calls mad. You will immediately be struck by the moderation and wisdom of his advice.

He will not begin by revealing to you the heights of glory to which his own transformed soul has attained; he will speak to you in a language suited to your weakness. He will not propose that you should imitate him; on the contrary, he will dissuade you from all excesses. He will not try to force upon you his own state of perfection; he will tell you to aim at that state of perfection which is yours — your very own. He will form a true estimate of your strength, a true estimate of all things. You will notice with astonishment that he understands human affairs a thousand times better than those do who spend their lives in transacting them. He knows the world a thousand times better than men of the world know it. Prejudice would have us believe that the Saints are dreamers, lost in the clouds, ignorant of everything. The contrary is the truth. The Saints draw from the very sources of Light a clearness of vision which embraces the most distant corners of the earth, the most obscure and the most forgotten.

If I needed a very practical piece of advice with regard to an extremely difficult and complicated matter, and if I were to hear that some St. Anthony had reappeared in the deserts of the East, I should go there and consult him.

To understand a matter properly, a man must dominate it, instead of allowing it to dominate him. Now, the ordinary man is dominated by a matter, but the Saints dominate the matter.

All men of good sense are not Saints, but all Saints are men of good sense. Good sense is in the midst of their sublime qualities, like a swimmer in the midst of the ocean. Look for it, and you will invariably find it.

If St. Teresa had been what rationalism and materialism would have us believe, she would have piled error upon error, folly upon folly; but it happens that she was skilful, shrewd, as prudent as she was ardent, and a good "man of business," if ever there was one.

The tree is known by its fruits. If, instead of being a Saint she had been an hysterical subject, Mount Carmel, far from producing fruits and flowers, would have disappeared under an avalanche of catastrophes.

Have you ever met with a lunatic who founded anything?

He who believes that the Saints are mad, is also obliged to believe in a sublime army of madmen who all agree together on the most exalted and delicate points of doctrine; in a vast army of orthodox, humble, kindly, peaceable, prudent, wise, cautious and discreet lunatics.

He is obliged to believe in lunatics who have the gift of counsel, and who foresee and avert dangers; in obedient lunatics, modest lunatics, philanthropic lunatics; lunatics who have thought, said, and done, the great things which sustain the life of humanity; lunatics who, instead of perishing in some catastrophe which reveals all too clearly their true condition, end their pure, wise, useful, courageous, and austere lives by calm, sublime, luminous, and fruitful deaths. He is, in fact, obliged to say good-bye to the most elementary principles of common sense, and to admit the absurd, simply in order that he may reject the supernatural.

XVI

THE WORLD

What is the world? This odious term seems to have no definite meaning, and yet it is odious. There are certain terrible statements in the Gospels, and among these statements this is one of the most terrible —"I pray not for the world[13]."

He Who speaks thus knows the inmost nature of things, and is about to die for sinners. He does not pray for the world, and it is St. John who tells us so. At the Last Supper, when his head was resting on the breast of Jesus Christ, at the solemn moment when the arms of God were about to be stretched out upon the Cross, it was then that St. John heard the Eternal Truth say, "I pray not for the world." You remember what is written elsewhere with regard to the lukewarm[14]. Without trying to enter into the full significance of these two declarations, I should like, looking at the world as it appears to us, to find out approximately what we mean when we speak of it.

Sin is confusion, disorder — self-evident, open, violent, disastrous disorder. But what is the world?

Can it be that the world is that part of the domain of Sin which is tempered by prudence?

Can it be that the world is that part of the domain of Sin co-extensive with the tepidity of the atmosphere?

The world extends as far as the tepidity of the atmosphere. Wherever the air is hot or cold, the world draws back scandalized.

The world has tastes and opinions; it has neither love nor hate. Its

---

[13] John 17:9.
[14] Reference to Revelation 3:16.

tastes are for those things which occupy an intermediate position. Its opinions dread to be absolute, and thus to resemble convictions. They have this peculiarity, that they do not exclude the contrary opinions. I say *opinions*; I do not say *convictions*. The opinions of the world fraternize willingly with other opinions of their own type. Whether these opinions are mutually contradictory or not, they get on equally well together, for one thing unites them — a deep-rooted dislike of their common enemy, Truth.

The world loves to mimic. It apes wisdom; it has invented a wisdom of its own, which resembles true wisdom as an orang-outang resembles man. True wisdom tends to unite. The wisdom of the world tends to amalgamate elements which cannot possibly be united, and when it has placed them in juxtaposition it believes that it has blended them.

The man of the world is not afraid of doing wrong, but he is afraid of giving offence. In the world, convention takes the place of harmony.

The world loves Evil, but loves it well-preserved, painted, decked out, and dressed according to the fashion. It loves Sin, but it likes Sin to be spruce and pretty and daintily clad.

The world is old. It is difficult to imagine how very old men of the world are. The young men especially are remarkable for their decrepitude, for in them it is more unnatural, and therefore more striking. Doubtless there is a secret way of remaining young, but this secret belongs to "God, Who is the Joy of our youth." God is the Master of Time, and when He speaks the word, Time stands still, like an ox petrified by a peal of thunder. Youth is a treasure which can only be confided to God, for no other arm is powerful enough to defend it.

Do not think that the spirit of the world is confined to those fashionable gatherings where it is generally supposed to hold sway. The drawing-rooms of the great, if they are animated by the breath of Life, may be free from the influence of the world and full of Truth; while the world may fill — and often does fill in its overflowing infamy — scores of lonely, deserted, inhospitable houses, cheerless hearths where there is no welcome for the stranger, hideous dwellings which refuse companionship and love to those who need them.

I remember a Breton fishing village where there are a few visitors in summer, and in winter nobody. On the lonely shore of this village I was talking one day with a peasant woman, and she confided to me the longing she had to quit "the world." I admired the depth of her remark and the true knowledge of the world which she possessed. For the world might well reign in her cottage, all the more hateful, perhaps, because the great ocean was so near. And the chatter of men would sound all the more insipid, since behind it she heard the solemn roll of the waves.

XVII

THE MEDIOCRE MAN

Is the mediocre man silly, stupid, idiotic? Not in the least. The idiot is at one extremity of the world, the man of genius is at the other. The mediocre man is in the middle. I do not say that he occupies the centre of the intellectual world, that would be quite another matter; he occupies a middle position.

The characteristic trait of the mediocre man is his deference for public opinion. He never really talks; he only repeats what others have said. He judges a man by his age, his position, his success, his income. He has the profoundest respect for those who have attained notoriety, no matter how, and for authors with a large circulation.

The mediocre man may have certain special aptitudes; he may even have talent. But he is utterly wanting in intuition. He has no insight; he never will have any. He can learn; he cannot divine. Occasionally he allows an idea to penetrate into his mind, but he does not follow its various applications, and if it is stated in different terms, he denies its truth.

The mediocre man may, and often does, respect good people and men of talent. He fears and detests Saints and men of genius — he considers them exaggerated.

Of what use, he inquires, are the religious Orders, especially the contemplative Orders? He approves of the Sisters of St. Vincent de Paul because their work relates, partially at least, to the visible world. But the Carmelites, he says, what can be the good of them?

The mediocre man admires everything a little; he admires nothing warmly. If you confront him with his own thoughts, his own sentiments, expressed with enthusiasm, he will be displeased. He will declare that you are exaggerating. He prefers enemies, so long as they are cold, to friends who are warm. What he detests above all is enthusiasm.

To escape the reproach of intolerance aimed by him at all who think with consistency and decision, you would have to take refuge in absolute doubt; but even then you must be careful not to call doubt by its name. You must represent it as a modest opinion, which respects the rights of the contrary opinion, and appears to affirm something while affirming nothing whatever.

The mediocre man, in his distrust of all that is great, maintains that he values good sense before everything. But he has not the remotest idea what good sense is. He merely understands by that expression the negation of all that is lofty.

The man of intelligence looks up to admire and to adore; the mediocre man looks up to mock. All that is above him seems to him ridiculous; the Infinite appears to him a void.

The mediocre man is much more wicked than either he himself or anyone else imagines, because his coldness masks his wickedness. He never gets in a rage. He perpetrates innumerable little infamies, so petty that they do not appear to be infamous. And he is never afraid, for he relies on the vast multitude of those who resemble him.

When, however, a man mediocre by nature becomes a true and sincere Christian, he ceases absolutely to be mediocre. He may not, indeed, become a man of striking superiority, but he is rescued from mediocrity by the Hand that rules the world. *The man who loves is never mediocre.*

XVIII

ENVY

Envy is the parody of Aspiration. Aspiration is that which is highest in man; Envy is that which is lowest. Aspiration is the eagle; Envy is the serpent. In our day, these two enemies are present; Aspiration hovers in the high, pure altitudes, while Envy crawls at the foot of the mountain.

In an age of tranquillity everyone occupies a definite place, determined by the position of his family, or, more rarely, by his own natural ability, but always determined by some known cause. In an age of restlessness, everyone aims at all things, fears all things, hopes all things. There are as many aspirants for supreme power as there are men in the world.

Finally, in an age of absolute restlessness such as ours, which is restlessness itself — unique, pure, unmixed restlessness — when ambition has assumed such vast proportions, when the power of rulers has diminished, when the deeper realization of human solidarity and the ever-increasing conquest of space make the earth seem like a single dwelling, there are as many candidates for the throne of the world as there are living men. Look at the various classes of human society; look at those who govern and those who are governed. They are all struggling at all costs to seize or to keep power. It would be unjust to reproach governments with this attitude. It is forced upon them by the nature of things and by the captious temper of those whom they have to govern. Whole nations, instead of seconding the efforts of those in authority after the physical, intellectual, and moral conquest of all that is good and beautiful, are turning against authority. The people are attacking authority, whether it go by the name of monarchy or republic, and they are attacking it not merely because they are discontented with what it does, but just because it is authority.

There are some faults which quickly attract the attention of man as soon as he has developed the moral sense. There are others which escape his attention. This phenomenon may be observed with regard to avarice and envy. It is also true of ingratitude and injustice.

Now, why this difference in man's attitude with regard to certain faults? We should have to travel far indeed to find a complete answer to the question, but a few observations naturally occur to us.

And first of all, faults which pass unperceived by the man who commits them have this character in common: they generally denote a base soul. Sins of passion are sometimes the errors of great natures. There are few great natures without a strong tendency to anger, and so men find it easy to acknowledge this tendency. A man is ready enough to say: "I am quick to anger, and unless I restrained myself I should be formidable." But he rarely, if ever, says: "I have an envious nature."

Envy is such a strong proof of inferiority that it draws back before an open avowal. The inferiority of which envy is the sign, is not merely a fault of conduct, it is an inferiority of nature, and it is much easier for a man to acknowledge that his will is corrupt than that his nature is corrupt. Who would dare to say even to an intimate friend, "Ingratitude is one of my leading characteristics"? Such a confession would resemble a disgrace. It would indicate not merely an accident of will, but a habit of mind, a type of character which one neither cares to acknowledge to oneself nor to others. For meanness always meets with contempt, and it is meanness and not guilt which man refuses to see in himself. Sins which are petty and mean displease him so much that he refuses to see them, even though they be staring him in the face.

And here may be noted a special property of sacramental confession: it gives to the man who speaks the strength to avow the unavowable, and it gives to the man who listens the strength not to despise him who avows himself despicable. Human things are here dominated by other and stronger forces, in virtue of which the impossible becomes possible.

To return to our subject. The envious man does not always insult others, sometimes he never insults them at all, but he speaks depreciatingly of that which is above him. His depreciation is expressed in moderate terms, and this very moderation gives to his opinion an air of probability. He disparages, but without violence; his disparagement is just enough to prevent admiration, or to kill it if it was about to spring up, but it is not marked enough to draw down upon himself suspicions which would weaken the force of his words. Admiration is, indeed, his personal enemy; there is only one case when, because he hates, he pretends to admire — and that is the case in which, in order that admiration should be withheld from the man who deserves it, he tries to procure it for the man who does not deserve it. Like all other creatures, the envious man has the instinct of self-preservation. He knows where the danger lies. And the danger lies where there is something superior, something admirable. When the envious man praises someone, it is not because he wishes him to be praised, but because he desires to diminish the reputation of someone else. "Doubtless, So-and-so is my friend," he says in effect, "but I do not allow myself to be blinded by friendship. I am quite ready to recognize his good qualities, but I consider it only right to point out where he is deficient."

The envious man is unprincipled, but he does not seem to be, and sometimes he does not even realize that he is. There are moments when envy disguises itself, and plays the part of candour. In its audacity it dares to seize and wear the mask of good-nature. The envious man is almost always what is called a good fellow, an amusing companion. Now, an amusing companion is very often volatile and superficial, and other men fall into the serious error of refusing to believe that he can be wicked. Yet what is shallowness but absence of heart? Superficiality is characteristic of all vices and crimes. Great villains are sometimes very volatile and superficial.

The typical envious man is obliging enough, and his companions will tell you that he is incapable of thinking evil, that he says all that comes into his head, it is true, but then he does everything he is asked to do. And you may hear these companions sum up their companion: "He's a pleasant fellow. Superficial? — rather. But bad? — impossible! *He* bad? What an idea!"

XIX

ON THE FALSE ASSOCIATION OF IDEAS

A man is rarely guided by conscious reasoning, true or false. The force which rules him is the association of ideas — an unconscious but powerful train of reasoning, by virtue of which one idea calls up another in his mind. Think of the people and things you have known; you will see that very often the picture you retain of them was not painted by reason but by imagination. Examine your memories, and you must confess that they are not founded on absolute justice: this man may have done you a bad turn, and yet you have a pleasant memory of him; that man behaved well, and you have forgotten him. It is the imagination which is the cause of this confusion.

You are, perhaps, accustomed to believe that crime may be a mark of greatness, that there are lies which are sublime, and that goodness is insipid. If you have not absolutely been taught these things, at least they have been suggested to you. They have not been openly put forward as truths to be accepted by your reason, but they have been insinuated in novels and plays, and your imagination has adopted them. If anyone should assert dogmatically that there is something grand in committing a crime, a young man would not believe him. But if in play after play you introduce the young man to criminals who are clever and interesting, and to honest men who are stupid and dull, he will form the *habit* of thinking that to be somebody, one must have done much evil in one's life.

Language, ever the accomplice of man, has certain expressions which bear terrible witness against him. When a young man's past is strewn with all sorts of folly, debts, lost opportunities, when he is inane, mediocre, useless and bored, people say that he has *seen life*.

They ought to say that he has *seen death*. What he has done is to do nothing. He has done nothing at all. He has allowed the void to ferment, and void has produced void. Then he has fallen a victim to *ennui*, and that is the end of the matter.

Whence comes this expression, *To see life?*

It comes from a false association of ideas. It comes from a latent lie. It has its source not in the reason, but in the imagination, which has formed the habit of associating the idea of Life with the idea of Disorder.

The imagination has lost the habit of associating the idea of the Beautiful with that of the Good. And when this happens, that which we see today ensues. When this habit is lost, men come to believe that Beauty and Purity are never to be found in the same country, and that it is necessary to choose between them.

XX

ART

Art is the remembrance of the universal presence of God. Art is Beauty expressed in ways that can be grasped by the senses. It is the form assumed by the Ideal under the laws of the natural world.

How shall it succeed in entering this land of exile?

Time and Space guard the frontiers of our world, and seize on all that enter. Nothing escapes them. And so Art condescends to submit its infinite and gracious splendour to human limitations. It does not violate its unity; but since the finite mind of man cannot grasp it as a whole, it reveals itself in different modes. Forced to submit to Time and Space, it begs their aid to help it to retain its beauty while it sojourns in the country which they rule. And Time lends it language, Space lends it light.

The laws of Time are summed up in arithmetic; the laws of Space in algebra. In the world of Art, arithmetic — the science of numbers — is the basis of poetry and music; for Time determines measure, and measure is rhythm. Geometry is the basis of architecture, sculpture, and painting, for it is Space which decides their proportions. Love is the life of Art, yet the arts are founded on mathematics, inflexible and absolutely exact. It is as though Love and Order, which men sometimes regard as opposed to each other, had determined to demonstrate their essential unity by the loftiest of their forms.

Art is an ascension. Its law is to rise. By its very nature it seeks the eternal types of things, and tends towards the Ideal. It may, indeed, lose sight of the Polar Star and make for a false ideal. Still, through every error we catch a glimpse of the Ideal, the corruption of which, in one way or another, explains the deviations of Art. Through every error we perceive the shattered form of Truth perverted.

Every artist — every artist worthy of the name — helps the human soul to breathe. Art, to a certain extent and at a given moment, is a force which blows the roof off the cave where we crouch imprisoned. What mighty levers does it employ? What massive weights have been placed at its service? Language! Music! A mere breath from human lips!

Poor fugitive notes, poor syllables caught away by the breeze! How invisible your majesty! How weak you seem! Yet you have power to shake earth to its foundations, and Heaven itself stoops to listen to you. In the solemn moments when we yield ourselves to your sway, our soul breathes a purer air; she breathes, and she is conscious of herself. She says: "Yes, my God, I am great, and I had forgotten it."

XXI

CONTEMPT FOR ART

There are certain feelings which men treat, as it were, with contempt. Now I call it treating a feeling with contempt when one abandons oneself to it without taking it seriously.

Among the feelings thus contemptuously treated is the feeling of Admiration.

Many men are not altogether unmoved by Beauty, but their very sensibility is an outrage, because they are not in earnest over it. If they hear or read or see something sublime, they are moved, and their emotion may even be demonstrative. But by next day there is no trace of it left. The business of everyday life has intervened, and there is not so much as a heap of ruins to show that Admiration has once been there.

The ordinary individual is convinced that Truth, Beauty, Harmony, are pretty fancies with which a serious man can amuse himself when he has finished his business. The Real, for such a man, is his profession, or trade. If, yesterday evening, he had time to admire, it was because his day's work was over and he had nothing better to do for the moment. He was therefore quite ready to give a few spare minutes to the things of Eternity. Do not, however, propose to him the following day to act upon the truths which the evening before restored youth and feeling to his soul. He would think you mad. When he goes to see a play, he is quite content that the heroine should be unhappy. He even enjoys her unhappiness for several very subtle reasons. But if next day, in real life, he were to come across a misfortune similar to the one he had been contemplating during the whole of the previous evening at the play, he would not even stop to look at it, because it would be no longer the time for laughter or for tears — it would be the time for business.

Now, this appalling contrast between the man as he is at a play and the man in real life, has wider consequences than you imagine. Every time you speak to such a man of Truth and of Beauty, every time you speak to him of the things of Eternity, it is to him just as though he were looking on at a play. Every time you speak to him of the Invisible, he believes himself at a play. For invisible things appear to him to have no reality, and are but, as it were, so much flimsy, artificial scenery you have chosen to introduce into your speech.

Contempt for Art is one of the commonest of sentiments, not only among ordinary men, but among artists and critics. To have a contempt for Art is to permit it to lie. The artist despises Art when he aims at anything but the realization of Truth. The critic despises Art when he pardons it for adopting an ideal which is not true.

Every day we hear this absurd expression with reference to some error clothed in brilliant language: "It is poetry." When the mediocre man, speaking of a lie, has declared that it is poetry, he thinks he has excused the liar. On the contrary, he has brought a fresh accusation against him; for if the liar lies *poetically*, he has laid hold of the loftiest form of language and forced it to utter a lie.

When the mediocre man desires to pander to the disorderly life of another man, he says: "He is an artist." If the man is really an artist, the disorder is most criminal. Music is founded on mathematics, poetry and painting depend on rigorous laws. Every artist should live in austere conformity to Order.

XXII

THE RIDICULOUS

The immediate effect of self-esteem is to render a person ridiculous. No matter from what quarter the wind may blow, flowers are never ridiculous. Animals never are, unless their nature has been purposely warped by man. Flowers and animals never pause to consider what effect they are producing, and herein lies the secret of their grace. When flowers bend before the wind, or deer spring swiftly forward, they are not posing before an audience. They are yielding to an impulse of movement, and they give no thought to any spectator who may happen to see them. They are admirable, because they fulfil their functions without any heed of us. They do what they were created to do, and never for a moment do they interrupt their actions in order that they may be seen. The lion bounding in the desert does not ask himself if there are any witnesses of his beauty; if he began to congratulate himself on his strength and agility, he would soon become stiff and affected.

Man aims at effect, and from this springs the ridiculous. Passion, even the most guilty passion, when it throws itself upon its prey without a thought of being admired, is not ridiculous. But the moment it begins to take pride in its violence — an odd phenomenon, but common enough in man — it adds to its crime the quality of being ridiculous. There is something ridiculous even in a man who performs a good action, if unfortunately he mingles with the most praiseworthy of motives a thought of self-esteem. You may save the lives of a whole crew in a shipwreck at the risk of your own life; but if, instead of abandoning yourself to the unmixed happiness of having been able to do such a deed, you desire to attract the attention of some spectator, then you will be more or less ridiculous. Even heroism does not suffice to banish ridicule. Simplicity alone makes it impossible. No one can ever be both simple and ridiculous. Any man who ceases to be simple immediately becomes ridiculous, do what he will and say what he will.

Even tears are ridiculous, if those who shed them appear conscious that they are being watched.

The simplicity of creatures has for its condition the abandonment of self-consciousness and self-esteem. This abandonment is peculiarly necessary in Art, which cannot exist apart from Beauty, The Art which allows itself to take applause into consideration abdicates its throne. It looks down instead of looking up. It places its crown on the head of the crowd. The figures in many a picture look as though they had nothing to do with each other, but were engrossed in the sight-seers strolling through the gallery. They are not thinking of what they are doing, they are thinking of us and looking at us; they are there for us, and not to accomplish the act they are represented as doing. This is often particularly noticeable in the pictures of children, with this strange and grievous result: Art makes children ridiculous.

XXIII

THE PRESS

In our day, Life and Death, which once were wont to clothe themselves in a more solemn guise, have discovered a way of entering our houses without ceremony. They slip in under a newspaper wrapper.

Two things characterize present society — curiosity and precipitation. People want to know, and they have not the time to study.

In former times, few people read, but those who did read, read in order to study. They read to be instructed, and in order that they might be able to instruct others.

Now, everybody reads, and they read in order to keep in touch with the men and things and facts of daily life.

The newspaper is the typical product of modern society.

Curiosity urges men to read.

Precipitation prevents them from reading anything long.

And the newspaper exactly meets the two needs of the multitude; men want to know and to know quickly.

The newspaper tells them what is happening, and satisfies their curiosity. It tells them in a few words, and thus satisfies their precipitation.

The newspaper comes again and again, and that is what men want nowadays. They like news to be frequent. They like to take in a succession of facts. They like the latest news, and, at the same time, they like all this successive information to reach them without any fatigue on their part, and to appear in their homes under a light and convenient form, materially accessible, and also intellectually accessible.

The newspaper answers these numerous requirements admirably. Its visits are frequent; its movements rapid; it weighs nothing. It circulates all by itself. It has feet. It has wings. It seeks people out in their houses. It gives them instruction at home, the light to enable them to see things clearly. The greater its influence, the more incumbent it is on it to use it in the service of great and true ideas. It must give to ideas their proper place by the side of facts. It must encourage all the high aspirations of readers and writers. It must open its pages to all that is great, and shut them to all that is petty. But it is absolutely necessary that its readers on their side consider their duties to their newspaper to be great and sacred duties.

Certain newspapers, because they flatter the passions, have on that very account a spicy flavour. They attract the eye by their striking colours. They excite a thousand ignoble desires. By this means they capture and hold public attention.

The good Press, on the other hand, sober and austere by nature, banishes from its pages all shameful elements, which in our day are also the elements of success. It bans a thousand descriptions, a thousand exaggerations, which have an attraction for vulgar and blasé minds.

And so it can only hope for support from those refined minds who love what is true and good; it can only retain the support of those who have kept their taste for beautiful things — and often beautiful things are more or less hidden things, which demand close attention if they are to be appreciated.

The conscientious and intelligent public must understand and realize that it is bound to love, support, assist, and encourage the healthy, courageous, and austere Press, as much as, and more than, the other public encourages the other type of Press.

The importance of the Press is one of those rare things which it is impossible to exaggerate. The Press sways public opinion with the same ease that the wind whirls away a dead leaf.

Just as truly as material bread forms flesh and blood, so, in this century of ours, the Press forms mind and soul.

The multiplication of writing is a veritable multiplication of loaves. Unhappily, poisons are multiplied as well as loaves.

However, the incontrovertible fact remains, that the Press nourishes the world. Familiarity, which has lessened our astonishment, cannot alter the astounding fact. The writing of one man carries Life or Death to the souls of innumerable men, who are separated from him by time and space, but subject to his influence through the multiplication of his written words.

From this it results that the invention of printing has created for every one of us a great and important duty. The duty is this: To bring Life within the reach of other men.

This duty, so simple, and at the same time so important, may be ranked among the forgotten duties.

If it were a duty we had rarely an opportunity of performing, we should perhaps be more conscientious about it. Printing, if it were rare, would alarm us by its power, but the very fact of its universality hides its importance from us. It has so successfully invaded our streets and our houses that we have ceased to perceive its gravity. This bread, just because it is daily bread, has lost its solemnity in our sight.

The Press is so familiar to us that we no longer detect Life or Death under the simple exterior that serves to veil them from our eyes. And yet they are there, all the more real because they are less apparent. They come to us all the more surely, because they come in so simple a form.

Circulate good books. These words, too simple to sound great, resemble a piece of advice in a commercial prospectus. And yet, without any glimmer of doubt, they are synonymous with these other words: *Circulate Life in the universe.* If we fail in distributing the word of Truth, we arrest the circulation of Life in the universe.

But as this is a sin of omission, honest people commit it without remorse. Man is prone to connect the idea of innocence with that of abstention. There are, however, abstentions which are crimes.

You look on, as you think, at some action apparently remote from you. One day, perhaps, you will be forced to recognize in yourself the author of that action.

Perhaps some inveterate reader of bad books and newspapers needed an antidote which it was your mission to procure for him. Perhaps you were the man who ought to have supplied him with daily bread instead of the daily poison he had been in the habit of taking. And perhaps some writer stood in need of this reader, as the reader stood in need of the writer. Perhaps, placed in communication, each would have helped and strengthened the other. Perhaps, apart, each is perishing at a distance from the other.

There are some meetings in life so useful, so truly wonderful, that they seem like visible interventions of Providence. Now there are certain men whose duty it is to procure for others such glorious meetings, and these men are those who have the control of the Press. Those who command the Press, those, too, who support it or who discourage it, open or shut the channels of communication by which people who were yesterday strangers may reach each other.

A certain man, driven by despair, blasphemes God and kills himself. He throws himself out of the window or into the river. Another man passes along the street, notices a crowd, and inquires with a kind of indifferent curiosity what is the matter. It is nothing, he is told, only some unhappy being who has made an end of his existence. And the passer-by goes tranquilly on his way, though he is perhaps ultimately the very man who has committed the crime.

Perhaps some book full of solid Truth, of real Beauty, contained the very words which the man needed in his temptation and his unhappiness, if only he could have read them in one of those decisive moments decreed by Providence when the soul is so easily swayed one way or the other.

But the book never reached him, and it was you, perhaps — you, the inoffensive passer-by — who ought to have put it into his hands.

Although they do not know each other, strangers are forever calling to strangers in the darkness and immensity of the night of the world. Those who control the Press are the organs of these mysterious voices. If we could perceive the invisible world, we should see hands stretched out, we should hear the moans of the poor in intellect, the cries of those who die of hunger. All this crowd of suppliants are pleading for bread, pleading for the word of Life.

There are loaves for them all, only they do not know it. The work of the printing-press is to multiply the loaves. And to you, all you good people, you honest people, to you is entrusted the starving populace. It is confided to your care.

You think, perhaps, that the propagation of such books and newspapers as set forth the Truth is a luxury. You are wrong: it is an absolute necessity. In all ages hunger has been a bad counsellor. It counsels the destruction of everything — of temples first, then of private dwellings. If you do not provide bread, men will eat poison, for there are those who prefer arsenic to the gnawing of hunger. If you do not provide bread, you will end by being devoured yourselves.

An army that feels itself to be victorious becomes invincible. It is the same with the battles of the intellect. The militant writer who feels himself to be victorious becomes invincible. The feeling of victory gives the attitude which alone renders victory possible. Now this victorious attitude, only the public can give to the writer; and the public, in the last resort, is each one of us.

Never let us forget that each one of us constitutes the public. We must not leave to others the sacred duty of encouraging and supporting those writers who have taken upon themselves to declare the Truth. Each one should say to himself in all seriousness:

> "*I am the public*. I am invested with formidable powers. Among all the books and newspapers offered to me, I choose. My choice is a judgment, a final judgment. Writers have to appear before a tribunal from which there is no appeal, and that tribunal is no other than I myself. Such and such a man who lives hundreds of miles away and whom I do not even know, is about to receive a sentence of life or death at the hands of the Press, and it is I who must pronounce the one or the other. For it is I who choose

whether bread or poison shall circulate in the world. It is I who have power to give to a certain writer, authority, encouragement, energy, eloquence, the courage to speak out difficult truths, and it is I who have power to deprive him of all these things. More than that: my powers extend farther still. Not only do I choose what shall be the nourishment of the present generation, but I choose that of the future."

So much for the general public. But there are also men who, on account of the very nature of things, on account of circumstances or position, are specially entrusted with the duty of pointing out to other men where to find the bread needed to sustain life and to take the place of poison. To them I say:

Official dispensers of human Speech, you must necessarily preside at the distribution of bread or the distribution of poison, at the distribution of Light or the distribution of Darkness. In God's name, choose well which it shall be!

XXIV

HISTORY

History is for humanity a recent glory; she was born not long ago. For centuries she was insignificant; afterwards she became a liar, without ceasing to be insignificant. Sometimes she forgot Truth altogether, sometimes she conspired against it. The conversion of the annals of man was reserved for the nineteenth century. Humanity, when it does not entirely reject Jesus Christ, often yields to the temptation of rejecting Him in part. When it makes room for Him, it is afraid of making too much room; when it respects Him in the tabernacle, it seems to say to Him: "You keep Your Church, and leave me Life, Science, air; leave me History — all those things do not concern You."

Humanity is tempted to believe that Our Lord is a stranger to the natural order, and that He ought to be content with His Will being done in Heaven.

The nineteenth century, however, which always strove to reach the heart of things, remembered — some times to blaspheme, sometimes to adore — that Jesus Christ is the Centre of History. It is impossible, indeed, to look anywhere and not perceive Him.

Whoever has travelled, whoever has wandered, must have noticed this: when the ground rises, when one reaches the top of a hill, when the view becomes extensive, the Cross appears. Church spires are the beauty of landscapes; their number is always important to the effect as a whole, even from the point of view of the picturesque.

Now, history is a mountain, from the summit of which man surveys the globe as it is in the present, and as it was in the past. It is the Cross which lights up this great landscape, and shows the traveller where he is and in what direction it behoves him to look.

History must, of course, know Time. Time is the domain of History, and must be grasped by her. Well, here is a very simple observation which I recommend to all thinkers, and which I beg them not to pass over lightly.

How, without Jesus Christ, would History reckon Time? If necessary, a nation could date its acts from its foundation as a nation, but what would nations do?

The age of Rome can be reckoned from Romulus. Greece can make use of the Olympiads, but who will provide a fixed and common measure for the life of peoples? It seems to me that every man capable of entering into the mysterious sense of life must be struck by this remark. History assumes the unity of the human race; she must embrace the whole world. How, without the Cross, could she embrace the whole world? She would be pulled up short at the first step by the most petty, yet most invincible of obstacles — by chronology. You will say perhaps: "But how did History manage before Jesus Christ? She had some mode of reckoning, I suppose."

And History will answer you, like the lamb in the fable: "How could I have done it, if I was not born?" For, mark well the Greeks and the Romans narrated their histories, but they did not write History. History supposes the universality of human relations; she is not obliged to enumerate them all, but she is obliged to suppose them all, and to assume the existence of those which she does not mention. If you write the History of France, you are not obliged to recount the History of India; but you are obliged to remember that India exists, that the human race is one, and that the actual sun is shining on Asia as on Europe in the present year of Grace. When the Romans wrote down the story of their acts, they were writing of their own particular affairs, but they were not writing the History of Man. Poets alone, in Antiquity, caught something of the majesty of History, because they looked beyond and above the walls of their city. But then poets were the mouthpieces of tradition — persistent though erring tradition — and what did all great tradition do but point to Him Who was to come? *Et ipse erit exspectatio gentium* [And to Him shall be the obedience of the peoples - Genesis 49:12] Israel had said. The echo of these words was in the air; and those who felt them vibrating over their heads, those who shared the great expectation, became participants in History, because in a certain way they entered into communication with the whole human race, and, by virtue of their desire, came out from behind their city walls. The ordinary historians, those who saw nothing beyond their own country, wrote memoirs — the memoirs of a city, not the annals of man.

The Jewish nation alone really made and wrote History, because to it was entrusted the task of preparing the way for universal salvation, and thus it was associated in a special manner with the designs of God. For this reason, its history is of equal interest to all people; it concerns them all, and instructs them all, for it announces and symbolizes Him Who came to call them all.

Sacred History speaks to us of ourselves and of every man. Her gaze is fixed on the future; she has her eyes on the Cross.

The Cross provided Space with a common measure applicable to Time.

And since then, History has become universal, and the nations of Antiquity have conquered their place in History, and won for themselves the rights of free citizens of the human family. They did not exist solely for themselves; they had an historic destiny, though they did not know it. They were in relation with us, though they did not know it. They only wrote their memoirs. It is for us to write their History.

History observes the nations of Antiquity and records their acts in proportion as these nations are employed by God to prepare the way for Jesus Christ. As soon as they cease so to act, History leaves them; and when the Jewish people have given first life and then death to the Saviour of the World, History moves away to cast the light of her lamp upon the nations towards whom the dying Christ stretched out His arms.

The Saviour is born; the world can no longer work at the formation of His physical Body in the same sense as before, but it is still working, and will work, at the formation of His mystical Body — the Eternal Jerusalem. Formerly, History looked towards the nations who were preparing the way for Jesus Christ; today, History still looks towards the nations who are preparing for Him. For He is our Head; we are His members, and He is waiting for us.

XXV

SCIENCE

Science is not a mere collection of various branches of knowledge. To be true, it must have the mark of peace, for it looks at everything from the point of view of Unity. Unity is the keynote of Science.

The huge edifice of Modern Science was begun much farther back than is generally supposed. I am far, of course, from maintaining that the Middle Ages achieved all there was to achieve. But we must be just to centuries as well as to individuals. In the Middle Ages, men did an immense amount of useful work; they penetrated deep into the nature of things. Finally, and this is their chief glory, they never looked at creation as a thing apart, isolated from the Creator.

It is precisely this alliance of the sciences with Science which earned for the Middle Ages the disdain of the last three centuries. The Middle Life, Science, and Art Ages have been turned into ridicule because then men spoke of God in connection with everything, and of everything in connection with God.

In modern times, it became the fashion to study Nature to the complete exclusion of her Author; to look upon her as detached and isolated, to probe her with material instruments, to examine her as one does an inanimate object, without respecting her or remembering her First Cause. Men came to believe that Science would be clearer and more exact, more profound and more authoritative, if they turned away their gaze from the skies and burrowed in the earth — far, far from God. They thought that they would find the reality if they abandoned the ideal, and gain in depth all that they lost in height.

Yet what is really the task of Science?

It is to search everywhere for the image or the traces of God. It is to discover and declare how He has endowed creatures with being —

though, unlike Him, they are not self-existent; how He has decreed that being should spring from them, since they transmit their forms to other beings — though, unlike Him, they are not creators. *Plena est omnis terra gloria ejus*! [The whole earth is full of His glory – Isaiah 6:3]. It is no high-sounding phrase, it is a reality.

We live in an age which hungers and thirsts after absolute completeness, and this can only be realized through the close union of Science and Religion.

The various sciences must be united to form true Science. And science must know, understand, realize, and proclaim, that Truth is one, and that Religion, being true, can neither contradict nor embarrass Truth. The unity of God must be clearly established. God never contradicts Himself; and since He is One; discord, confusion, anomalies and contradictions are absolutely impossible.

Is it not a fact that the law of solidarity lies at the root of all modern discoveries?

True science goes beyond and supersedes the systems devised by man. It knows things as they are, not as the human mind loves to arrange and explain them; it knows them as God has made them, and not as man has dreamed them to be.

Creation is an inclined plane, a ladder that leads to the skies. Man, body and soul, is the connecting link between the visible and the invisible. All things bear witness to God; the smallest among His creatures please Him already, but the greatest are not yet conformed to His image; the Heavens tell His glory, *et sanctum nomen ejus.* [And holy is His name – Luke 1:49].

XXVI

THE HOLY SCRIPTURES

The Holy Bible is an abyss. It is impossible to explain how profound it is, impossible to explain how simple it is. If one of these two things surprised me, it would be not so much the profundity as the simplicity. I should expect the Bible to be profound, but man is so complex that he does not expect it to be simple. The words of the Gospels, repeated to a child, a workman or a peasant, do not surprise him in the least. Nothing is told with a view to effect. Not a word in the Gospels is intended to startle. Our Lord speaks almost exclusively in natural and familiar language; the objects which He names most frequently are the objects of everyday life. Rural life, daily work, the flowers of the field — these are the things which play a large part in His discourse, whereas what we may term the *scientific* element is wholly wanting.

The child, the workman and the peasant, find nothing surprising in the Gospels.

But when these same words — so simple that they overwhelm the human mind — become the daily food of thinkers, philosophers, theologians and Saints, then these feel the astonishment that children do not feel. They discover that these same simple words are so full of knowledge and depth that no one can ever fathom them. The longer one meditates on them, the more clearly one perceives how necessary it is to go on meditating. And the more one understands, the more one realizes how far one is from understanding. The ignorant man thinks he understands, and he is not altogether mistaken, for he can understand something. The man of genius who has passed his life in the study of the Holy Scriptures, every day perceives more clearly that they have not yet told him all their secrets, and in this he is not in the least mistaken.

There is something in the Mosaic Books which fills us with especial awe. Everything is recounted, as it were, in the same tone, no matter whether it be the creation of the world or the follies of a man. Nothing appears to astonish the narrator. We never detect the slightest start of surprise. It is as though he looked at everything in a uniform light and saw all things reduced to a point: never once does his voice rise or fall. He gives us the impression of having everything within range of his hand, so that with a gesture he could reach the farthest limits of the universe. Whether the Holy Bible is speaking of the stars of Heaven or the dunghills of earth, it is equally at its ease; it dominates everything with the same serenity. It is never embarrassed or constrained; heights offer no difficulties to it, neither do precipices. Its outstretched wings embrace everybody and everything. In its sovereign calm, it seems to say to the stars: "Humble yourselves! there is Someone above your heads." It seems to say to the dust: "Arise! there is Someone Who with a touch can make you glorious."

As a general rule, language troubles the solemn silence which reigns at times — which can reign, at all events — between God and man. Silence includes all things in its mysterious depths. It does not reason and define; it is at peace; it rests, and it understands. As a general rule, language troubles this silence. It would wrest its secret from it — it would probe its hidden depths. The Holy Scriptures, on the contrary, do not trouble the silence of the soul, for the language they speak is deeper even than silence. Through their words we detect, as it were, a silence which resembles the voice of the night — a silence which breathes in the Old Testament the name of Jesus and of His Mother.

The simplicity of the words of the Bible — above all, the simplicity of the words of Our Lord — are of the deepest import, not only from an intellectual point of view, but from the point of view of practical action. Virtue goes out from these words; they are not only simple, they are simplifying. They communicate simplicity. Men of genius, who have such great need of simplicity, should drink from this source.

For indeed men need more than genius if they would understand the words of God. Faith and recollection of spirit are absolutely essential. Genius, both in itself and by reason of the human nature to which it is attached, would be liable to all kinds of error if it started off alone to explore the Holy Scriptures at random, far from the Church and from the Faith.

We must have Faith; we must have simplicity. We must remember that the Church, the Bride of Christ, is the guardian, interpreter, and depositary of His treasures.

If we would understand Divine things, we must cultivate an attitude of humble adoration. Whoever does not begin by kneeling down, runs every possible risk.

XXVII

THE HOLY ANGELS

There are a thousand ways of uttering and hearing the word faith. There is a dead faith and a living faith. A dead faith is satisfied with formulas, but a living faith draws down to us an objective Reality.

Many good and devout Catholics believe in the Saints of Paradise with a living faith. But those whose faith in the Angels is a living faith are much rarer.

It is easier to believe in the Saints, because they once lived on the earth, and men believe in the earth. The Saints possess a visible, historical, external reality, and thus up to a certain point they force themselves on the attention of men. But the Angels, whose history is celestial, receive little attention. The inhabitants of earth are prone to look upon the inhabitants of Heaven as scarcely existing, scarcely capable of occupying a serious place in the minds of serious men — sensible men of business who are accustomed to speak in prose.

This way of looking at things, involuntary and unconscious though it often be, is radically opposed to faith.

The Saints look at the invisible world with quite other eyes.

The Saints firmly believe in the Holy Angels, and love them with an active and personal love. Read the lives of the Saints, and you will see that the Angels had a share in every detail of their existence, in their business, their interests, their conversation. Their conversation was in Heaven[15]. It is what St. Paul wishes for all of us; and certainly we must leave no small place in our lives for the Angels, if we would carry into practice these inspired words.

Decidedly, the Angels play a great part in the lives of the Saints, a

---

[15] Philippians 3:20,21.

great part in the Holy Scriptures.

The Bible seems to desire to draw our special attention to the Angel Raphael. It encourages us to invoke him, and the way in which it does so is as follows:

In the Book of Tobias, it shows us an abyss of unhappiness and an abyss of happiness; it tells us how Raphael appeared to the famous family of Tobias, and led them by the hand away from their sadness into the peace and the glory of Joy.

It appears that Joy is the special province of Raphael; that everything to do with Joy — its circumstances, its incidents — has been directly confided to him. *It would seem that God has appointed the angel Raphael His minister for the province of joy.*

And as it is impossible to know how much the human soul needs Joy, so it is impossible to know with what confidence men would turn to the Angel Raphael, if they really believed with a living faith in his existence, his action, his influence, his efficacy.

Men often talk of "chance." They would do well to replace this sacrilegious word by the name of the Angel Raphael.

Tobias and his family were the victims of the most cruel circumstances of human destiny.

Holy Scripture shows us the old man, blind, and encompassed by darkness, and by sadness as deep as the physical darkness. In addition to this, he has to bear the grief of separation from his son. For the young man is obliged to undertake a long journey — a journey necessitated by a matter of business. Sombre necessity, indeed! which constrains him to leave his father — sad, blind and old — and to go to a strange and distant country on a matter of business.

If ever circumstances called for the presence of the Angel Raphael, they were surely these. And the Angel Raphael came.

Young Tobias, son of the blind man — and blind himself with regard to his destiny, which was about to be arranged by an Angel — young

Tobias obeyed his unknown guide, and because he obeyed, his path was made smooth before him.

The Book of Tobias is eminently calculated to reveal the Hand of God in human affairs.

The horizon was threatening indeed! The very marriage of the young man offered a thousand menaces; the grave seemed about to open at his feet. In any case, his marriage, never probably to be brightened by an approving glance from his old father's eyes, seemed sad as death. But the Angel Raphael was there, and sadness vanished away like mist at sunrise.

By his journey, the young man accomplished all that he had intended, and he also accomplished a thousand other things of which he had never thought.

Who can count the catastrophes which follow one on the other, when a man neglects or rejects an Angelic inspiration? And what eye can follow the series of glorious events reaching from earth to Heaven, which owe their rise to successive Angelic inspirations, perseveringly listened for, and faithfully obeyed?

We are all such travellers that it seems specially fitting we should invoke the Angel Raphael. Since the days of the tents of the Patriarchs, man has been a traveller. It is a mere platitude to repeat this; still, in our time, this truth, by the sheer force of its truth, is fresher than ever.

Our century is an army on the march.

Every life is a journey. No one has a home. If men seem to settle down, it is only *seeming*. The hour of departure strikes incessantly.

O Raphael, lead us towards those we are waiting for, those who are waiting for us!

Raphael, Angel of Happy Meetings, lead us by the hand towards those we are looking for! May all our movements, all their movements, be guided by your Light and transfigured by your Joy. Angel guide of Tobias, lay the request we now address to you at the Feet of Him on

Whose unveiled Face you are privileged to gaze. Lonely and tired, crushed by the separations and sorrows of earth, we feel the need of calling to you and of pleading for the protection of your wings, so that we may not be as strangers in the Province of Joy, all ignorant of the concerns of our country. Remember the weak, you who are strong — you whose home lies beyond the region of thunder, in a land that is always peaceful, always serene, and bright with the resplendent glory of God.

XXVIII

ALONE AND POOR

"Look thou upon me, and have mercy on me; for I am alone and poor."
— Ps.24: 16.

Alone and poor!

There are moments when man perceives his misery for the first time. I ought perhaps to say: There is a moment. Then I can proceed to add, for the first time. But no! There are moments, there are many moments, when man perceives it for the first time.

Some time ago he perceived it; some days ago he perceived it; today he perceives it, and again it is for the first time. So deep is the abyss of his misery that over and over again he can perceive it for the first time. What he saw ten years ago was not what he saw last year; and what he saw last year was nothing compared with what he saw yesterday; and what he saw yesterday was nothing compared with what he sees today.

So deep is the abyss of human misery that whenever we look into it we may be said to see it for the first time. It is unfathomable, and we may sound it again and again, yet never reach the bottom.

When man, armed with his poverty, comes into the presence of God, I do not know when he can possibly say, "I have shown everything."

But this he can say: "Look! Look at all that I show Thee. Look, too, at all that I do not show — all that I do not even know how to show. Thou before Whom hell is naked, to quote the words of Job, look at my wretchedness, and have pity on me; look at the misery of which I am conscious, and the misery I do not even perceive."

XXIX

THE FRIENDS OF JOB

The friends of Job are immortal and truly wonderful types. They are not wanting in intelligence, they are only wanting in heart, but because they are wanting in heart, they cannot understand, and their intelligence — which yet is so quick, lucid, logical, alert, and open — deceives them absolutely. A little more heart would have enabled them to see. Their thoughts appear pious, sensible, and probably true; an air of reasonable probability characterizes all their remarks. The word *probable* together with the word *severe* are perhaps the expressions which describe their attitude the best. They have an answer for everything. They are often disconcerting; they are never disconcerted. An apparent piety presides over all they say. And everything is hidden from them.

One flash from the heart would light up the horizon, which is absolutely dark as far as they are concerned.

They say so much that sounds likely, so much that sounds severely just, consistent, and sober, that there is nothing to say in reply. Nothing? Just one word, perhaps: "I was hungry, and you gave Me not to eat; I was thirsty, and you gave Me not to drink."[16]

And yet this supreme reproach does not, in its strictest sense, apply to the friends of Job. They visited the sick man, and their first impulse was good. They began by weeping. Blinded by their reasoning, they did not follow the guiding light of the heart. But they had begun by weeping, and God forgets nothing. At the beginning of the book they wept, and at the end of the same book, God, Who takes account of everything, but beyond and above all of tears — God, Who might, perhaps, be called the God of Tears — tells Job to pray for them, because, in answer to the prayer of Job, He desires to pardon the friends who had begun by weeping.

---

[16] Matthew 25:42

XXX

"CREDO, DOMINE: ADJUVA INCREDULITATEM MEAM."

"The father of the boy cried out with tears: I believe, Lord; help my unbelief." — Mark 9:23.

What singular words! They are a contradiction in terms. Does he who speaks thus believe, or does he not believe? He is a man — this is the answer.

What sincerity in his contradiction, and what a longing that his prayer should be heard!

All things are possible to him that believes, Our Lord had said. I believe. This is the first word of the reply. Since all is possible to the believer, then I believe. The man begins by affirming his rights, presenting his title-deeds. It is the cry for help, the cry of hope, the bold request.

Then comes the timid request.

I believe. It was the first cry of a man who wished to obtain. But reflection follows — reflection and awe. He who has just said *Yes*, now says *Perhaps*.

I believe. But do I believe firmly enough? Do I really believe? Do I believe with a serious, real, true and perfect faith? Is my faith that all-powerful faith of which He Whom I implore has just spoken?

Oh, I know nothing at all about it. What shall I do?

All I can do is to appeal to Him for faith, as I have already appealed to Him to heal my son. He says that if my child is to be cured, I must believe. Well, as I do not know what to do either to cure my child or to make myself believe, I will ask both faith and healing of Him Who can give both.

Our Lord had just come down from Tabor, where he had vouchsafed to three of His Apostles a glimpse of His glory[17]. As they descended the mountain, He told them to keep silence about it until the Son of man should be risen from the dead. And they questioned together what this meant. Perhaps they were surprised at the thought of death in connection with Him Whom they had just seen in such glory on Mount Tabor.

Our Lord had not forgotten death on Mount Tabor, but the others had perhaps forgotten it. A few minutes afterwards, a man brings to Our Lord his son, who has a dumb spirit. He had taken him first to the disciples, but they had not been able to cast out the spirit.

Then follows one of those interrogations so frequent in the Gospels. Our Lord asks questions about what He knows. He gets people to relate and explain things which He knows much better than they do themselves.

The father describes the frightful condition of his son. He tells it with perfect simplicity, without any embarrassment or circumlocution.

Under the pressure of great unhappiness, human speech loses its reticence. The father speaks of things just as he sees them — just as he has always seen them ever since his boy was an infant. The spirit throws itself upon the child, who gnashes his teeth and foams at the mouth; sometimes it casts him into the water, sometimes into the fire.

"If Thou canst do anything," concludes the father, "help us — have pity on us!"

We feel that we have here a man who can bear no more, who hardly knows where he is, who catches at a last hope, without knowing what reception he will get.

"If Thou canst do anything!" The *if* is so heart-rending. Who knows what efforts this man has made to catch hold of this last hope!

To this *if*, Jesus Christ replies by another *if*. "If thou canst believe, all

---

17   The Transfiguration, recounted in Matthew 17:1-13.

things are possible to him that believes."

And immediately the father of the boy cries out with tears: "I do believe. Lord; help my unbelief!"

In his naive distress and longing, in his piteous prayer, he gives no thought to making his words consistent. He does not ask himself if they will be handed down to others. He does not think of posterity; yet, little as he dreams it, posterity will listen to him. In one and the same breath he says *Yes* and *No*. What could be more human? He says that he believes and that he does not believe. He calls for help — help in his great need. He wants to make the most of the moment while the Master is there, and he says just what is necessary for the healing of his son. Without stopping to weigh his words, he says exactly what is required to excite pity, and also to fulfil the condition laid down.

I believe, means — here especially — *I want to believe, I have the will to believe.*

This most human cry — this cry so full of longing and of contradiction — is accompanied by something else, by something that is perhaps more human than anything else, more human even than speech: it is accompanied by tears.

Tears play an immense role in the pages of the Holy Scriptures. What is more mysterious than tears? Is not the union of soul and body made clearly manifest by this physical phenomenon — a phenomenon which expresses outwardly all that is deepest and sincerest, most private and most touching, in the inward feelings of the heart? Tears are the sign of weakness, and for this reason they are always given in the Bible as the sign of power. Is it necessary to repeat it? Tears are, perhaps, of all human things the most irresistible. At every instant — almost invariably — the Holy Scriptures, in telling us of a prayer that has been granted, point out that he who prayed wept while he was praying. It is as though this supreme weakness were productive of strength. Tears disarm the strong; they admit of no reply.

The father, then, weeps, and Jesus orders the unclean spirit to go out of the child, and not to enter into him anymore. This last direction is not needless, for nothing is given needlessly in the Bible. Note the importance of shutting the door when the evil spirit has gone.

The child appears as if dead. He is freed, but he seems dead.

Our Lord takes his hand and lifts him up, and the child lives.

Through these brief details, let us try to follow the drama. What is it that has just happened to the boy? He has been the theatre where terrible scenes have taken place. Thrown into the water, thrown into the fire, foaming at the mouth, he is brought to Our Lord.

His father weeps. The demon, deaf and dumb though it be, hears the order given. The violence of what then takes place seems to throw the child into the very arms of death.

Then the Hand of Jesus touches him.

The child stands up, and there is no mention of him anymore.

Once the Hand of Our Lord is stretched out, the drama is at an end. The apparent death is vanquished, just as the real possession has been vanquished. All is over.

For the Hand of Jesus is there.

XXXI

WORK AND REST

A year is ending; another year is about to begin. This, then, is the moment to renew our youth: *Adveniat regnum tuum!* [May your kingdom come.] We shall grow young to the sound of the bells that are ringing the flight of Time, if we follow the star which appeared to the Three Wise Men. We shall grow young, if we leave behind us the trivial things, which are always old, and live in the Infinite; if we bring our Science and Art to the feet of Eternal Beauty, which is also Eternal Youth, *ad Deum qui Icetificat juventutem meam* [God Who makes my youth happy].

You will grow young again, all you who complain of time, at once tedious and rapid for you, on the day when you definitely devote yourselves to the interests of Truth on this earth, and decide to fight on its side. We shall all grow young again, if we can obtain from God and from ourselves two things — things which we ask of God and which He asks of us: Work and Rest.

To work is simple enough; but to rest, there is the difficulty. We crave for work, but rest demands an effort. Man works without repose when he acts depending only on himself; he both works and rests when he acts depending primarily on God.

"Without Me you can do nothing," said Jesus Christ.

Which of us can obtain by his own strength a moment of life? As well count upon the force of our little finger to launch a planet in space, as undertake a work in our own strength, as contend unaided with Nature and Humanity. Yet, marvel of marvels! the action of man may be united to the action of the Self-existent. Every human act, even the most impotent, loses its impotence when united to the Act of Redemption. God grants to us, and even commands us to accept, the glorious productiveness of an activity united to His own. We act in Him, and our very work is repose in Him.

www.ingramcontent.com/pod-product-compliance
Lightning Source LLC
Chambersburg PA
CBHW020147170426
43199CB00010B/922